When the Bond Breaks

Separation, Divorce and Remarriage

Esly Regina Carvalho, Ph.D.

Plaza del Encuentro

Plaza Counseling and Training Services
info@plazacounselingservices.com

Title: **When the Bond Breaks: Separation**, Divorce and Remarriage

© 2014 Esly Regina Carvalho

ISBN-13: 978-1-941727-06-5
ISBN-10: 1941727069

Originally published in Portuguese by Editora Ultimato: *Quando o Vínculo se Rompe* (2000).

Published in Spanish by Ediciones Kairos, *Cuando se rompe el vínculo* (2005)

Plaza del Encuentro

Plaza Counseling and Training Services
www.plazacounselingservices.com
info@plazacounselingservices.com

Cover: Claudio Ferreira
Translation into English: Esly Regina Carvalho

Table of Contents

Table of Contents...3

Preface...6

Introduction...8

Single Again: On Emotional Recovery 10

Separation and Divorce 18

The Pain of Divorce..26

Her Lamp Does Not Go Out at Night 30

Life Goes On…..32

And When You Miss Him…? 36

My Son Is Getting a Divorce… 38

Who Gets to Keep the Friends? 42

Divorced, Yet Friends: Is this really possible?...................44

Is Reconciliation Possible?..48

A Christian Woman and Divorced 54

A Virtuous Woman: Who can Find?...................................56

The Church and the Divorced 60

Shall We Marry Again?..66

God is a Matchmaker 70

Divorce, the Law and Jesus, By Walter L. Callison 76

About the Author 86

Other books (in English), by Esly Carvalho:.....................87

Preface

As a Christian psychiatrist I have treated hundreds of people suffering through divorce and its enduring consequences. Divorce is a very traumatic experience. As professionals we do all we can to prevent divorce, including individual or joint marriage counseling; but sometimes divorce is forced upon people, and sometimes it *is* the best option. The same God who created marriage also created divorce for certain circumstances. Some church denominations have trouble dealing with divorce and some people find it is easy to discriminate against those who have been through the pain of divorce. It is interesting to note that psychological research has shown divorce to be even more painful and traumatic than the pain caused by the death of a beloved mate. Divorce brings feelings of rejection and many other complications that go above and beyond the pain that results from the loss of a spouse by death.

I have personally known and worked with Dr. Esly Carvalho for many years now and highly regard her both as a therapist, and as a compassionate and wise human being. I am so very happy that she wrote *When the Bond Breaks*. This book will help many thousands of people who read it, as well as their loved ones, with whom they can share the principles found here. The book thoroughly covers all the stages a person goes through during the divorce process, and even covers what happens following the divorce, including the post-divorce dating and remarriage process. Esly gives advice for those who feel rejected by legalistic church members who discriminate against the divorced. She covers all the bases.

Those who find themselves in the process of divorce can help prevent a great deal of the pain by reading this book. Knowing what to expect at each stage prepares the victim of divorce for what lies ahead, and -allows the divorcing person to pray for guidance and be prepared, not shocked, by the changes ahead. Hopefully, this book will also help its many readers go through the process in a way that is less painful, especially for the children involved, and for the extended family members and friends of the divorced.

I highly recommend this book.

Paul Meier MD, Founder of the Meier Clinics

Introduction

This book was originally written in Portuguese, many years ago (2000), and published in Spanish as well. It came together from different sources, but basically, from people who asked me to write about the difficult issues that one deals with when facing a divorce.

Having gone through a divorce myself, and going through my own journey of faith through it all, much of what I wrote was based on my own personal experience. It also reflects much of what was going on, and unfortunately, still goes on in Latin America, although I believe it is also relevant to a North American audience.

This is a compendium of articles written over a period of several years. Besides the practical everyday situations that one faces when going through a divorce, herein is included the story of how I eventually remarried, since everybody asks, smile… it is highly autobiographical, but I believe that many of my own experiences reflect a lot of what others (especially women) go through navigating these difficult waters.

At the end of this book is an article, reprinted by permission of Rev. Walter L. Callison, on the issue of remarriage. (Callison wrote a book, entitled, *Divorce: a Gift of God's Love,* by Leathers Publishing [2002] for those who would like to read further about his ideas.) Callision brings a refreshing understanding through an academic study of the passages on divorce from their original languages. More than anything, he brings divorcees hope: that divorce is not the unpardonable sin and that we are not second-class citizens, doomed to a life of loneliness because of what oftentimes was the result of someone else's sinful decision.

Finally, there are many people I would like to thank because they contributed to the development of this book, but for fear of leaving someone out, I shall refrain. You know you who are.

...Except for one special person, my daughter, whom I thank for letting me share what essentially became our story. Thank you for who you are in my life.

Esly Carvalho, August, 2014

Single Again: On Emotional Recovery

Having the opportunity to write on this subject some years after my divorce has given me a unique chance to reflect on and organize some of the experiences that I went through as God brought me closer to wholeness. It was a relatively simple process, but certainly not an easy one. Today I can honestly say that life is full of unexpected turns in the road, but that we can learn to greet these surprises as exercises in growth and not as something that would utterly destroy us.

On loss

My marriage had been going downhill at a brisk pace by the time my daughter turned two. Less than a year later it was over. This was a terrible time in my life, a time of many losses. I had never thought about how much one loses in a divorce until they began to arrive: I lost my husband (obviously), my marital status; I also lost his daughter by his first marriage that had come to live with us after the birth our child. She was twelve by then and had become an integral part of my life. I had to leave the house we had lived in, the neighborhood, and those friends that had surrounded us in so many ways. A month after he had left I discovered I was pregnant and with the discovery came the miscarriage and all of the conflicting feelings related to that experience. Having refused to consider an abortion (besides, it is illegal in Brazil), I lost the baby before I ever really made the adjustment to maternity. And yet, when I saw my best friend wearing my maternity clothes that I had given her months before, I burst into tears...

Even the dog died. It was a time of death and dying.

Ecclesiastes speaks of a time to live and a time to die (Ecc. 3). This was certainly my time of death. So much died but much more died within me. When I left the hospital after the miscarriage I realized that the love I had had for my husband had died with the baby. My hopes for reconciliation after that were also dead. I didn't want the marriage to recover and I prepared to confront life alone.

If there was one emotion that defined this period of my life it was ambivalence: ambivalence about the situation that I found myself in, towards my husband, my friends, my church, and towards God.

Back then, I wasn't certain that I could ever be comfortable with the idea of being a divorced woman. It wasn't a role I had ever intended to learn and it went against so much of what I had wanted for myself and expected out of my life. But I had to admit that it was certainly here to stay whether I wanted it or not. On the other hand, the relief that was offered by the separation had something to be said for it. In the last months of my marriage, there was so much fear present that not having to be so constantly afraid was a definite improvement. It was a fragile relief, almost like a respite, yet I could see that perhaps one day it could even be turned into a lasting peace instead of a temporary truce.

My feelings towards my husband were also very ambivalent. How could I hate and fear someone with whom I had fallen in love and promised to love and cherish forever? I had had a child with this man, such a special experience, and now she had become one more bone of contention. How could I be so mad at him? Yet I knew that he was still important to me. My well-meaning friends would sometimes poke fun at me, implying that I still loved him. At first, I would defiantly deny it. With time, I owned up to the fact that it was very difficult to cut someone who had been so important to me out of my life at the drop of a hat. I understood that a divorce meant reversing the direction of intimacy: when we were first married, we worked at developing intimacy. With the separation, I was going to have to work at making him become a stranger again.

I was also ambivalent with my friends and towards my church. I knew that I certainly needed them, but I was very much aware that I had to risk their rejection to gain their support. I was very blessed in this period of my life by some special people who saw me through it all. One fine Christian woman prayed me through the difficult weeks and months that ensued. She has earned my eternal gratitude for her listening and her prayers. I am sure that I bored her to tears, yet she held in there and let me lean on her as I needed it.

Other people helped. One pastor would call every two weeks and leave me a little message on my answering machine just to let me know that he was thinking of me and should I need him to please call. I still remember that with gratefulness. There was also a small church that took me in. Nobody asked any snoopy questions, yet I knew that I could ask them to pray with me and that they would stand with me. The divorce changed nothing in our care for each other. I realize now that it was an added blessing.

The losses had been tremendous. No wonder I always felt that my stores of energy had been depleted. I understood that I was working through these losses. I often let myself cry when I felt overwhelmed. It didn't solve any problems, but I felt better afterwards. Years later, when I began to work in Latin America, training facilitators in emotional recovery in the face of great losses resulting from natural (and "unnatural") disasters (earthquakes, wars, civil strife, landslides, etc.), I perceived that God had guided my steps through my own process. Intuitively (or was it the Holy Spirit?), I had given myself permission to feel the enormity of my losses and mourn them. There are no funerals for divorce or any other adequate or socially-accepted rituals to mourn it. To the contrary, it is often whispered on tiptoe in woeful tones of pity, as if it were something shameful of disgraceful. Crying is a healing part of recovery and I often saw that my patients who didn't cry their losses took much longer to recover and often had to be encouraged to do so.

I was still very much afraid of rejection. I didn't get involved in church programs, went to very few meetings, spoke little, hoping to pass by unnoticed and thereby accepted.

Most of all, I was ambivalent towards God. I really couldn't understand how a God of love, harmony and reconciliation was letting my marriage come crashing down around my ears. I thought it was up to God to keep it together, not let it fall apart. I was upset with God for a good while, and yet, I needed the Holy Spirit so desperately: for comfort, wisdom, consolation and hope. God was my all and all, and in God's arms I often cried myself to sleep.

Many people had often commented on how God had helped them through the more difficult parts of life. Now it was my turn to realize the truthfulness of God's presence. There were so many things with which I felt that I couldn't cope. Simple things were a horrendous effort when I had to do it all in the midst of an immeasurable depression. But I began to find God faithful in a new way. The money for the rent always came in. The patient-load at the office increased without any effort on my part. And we had peace at home.

I spent one year mourning my losses. Life was always gray. I laughed very little. My ex-husband and I cried over the phone at Christmas when we recalled that the little baby should have been born about then.

And then, one day, life began to recover its colors.

Convalescence

In part, this process began side-by-side with the mourning, but it was so infinitely difficult to see it that only when the loss had been properly worked through did I understand that it had begun much earlier.

This was the healing phase, the "let's get on with life" time. It was hard to mend what had been broken, salvage the good, and toss out what was worthless. It also had its' humps, but good things began to come out of the pain. I heard my daughter laugh her delicious giggle for the first time six months after the divorce was finalized. I cried because I realized how long it had been since I had heard it, but I heard it, and I knew that her winter snow was beginning to melt.

I spent a lot of time thinking during this period, perhaps even more talking it out. I did some therapy, which helped. I prayed that God would change me so I wouldn't make the same mistakes again. I made monumental decisions that have had consequences into the present and for which I am grateful. I decided to make the best life possible for my daughter and me. We were a family, reorganized, non-traditional, but a family. We were going to have a home, not a house. God was going to be the head of the household, the father, the husband. I read Proverbs 31:10 until I could recite it by heart. "Who says only married women are 'virtuous'?"

Virtue was not something I figured I derived from my civil state. So I tried to write my first book, but had to stop halfway because of the emotional hemorrhage. I wasn't well enough to finish, but I was well enough to start.

I began to go out and do things. I started my Master's degree. Knowing how hard I could be on myself, I made a promise to start, but that I would stop when I felt that I couldn't go on, or when my daughter needed me more than the books. (They kept me company on the weekends she was off with her dad. It also helped ease the pain of the empty bedroom. She was only four by then...) I graduated three years later with a thesis on family structure.

I made new friends. I hung on to some of my "married" friendships, but they usually had different schedules, lived far away, or had moved on to other things. Some of them backed away from me, but most simply lost their meaningfulness. Others had been "his" friends to begin with.

I discovered I had a new freedom to come and go. Some days I was more "married" than single, like when I had my daughter with me, needed a babysitter, or I couldn't find a place to leave her after school so that I could keep on working. But other times, I was "single again", and I had never thought that the solitude could become company. I began to like being alone. I discovered it didn't necessarily mean loneliness. It was a fun time, when I began to appreciate my own company, but in small doses initially. I couldn't take it all at once. I would read a book, listen to the music I liked, eat when I felt like it, do my papers for school, or sleep in the middle of the afternoon (more and more out of tiredness and less and less out of depression.) When I got tired of myself, I'd call up a friend and go out somewhere.

Life began to bloom out in new colors.

Moving on

As life began to take on new colors, so did I. I wore red, not black; bright green, not dead grays. Life was beginning to get interesting and each day brought new challenges and not just another chapter in the Survivor's Manual of Life. I was beginning to realize that there *was* life after divorce.

What was most intriguing, I realized that it was a great life. Surviving was not all there was to it. Perhaps because I also became a more interesting person, I got invited to do things I had never done before. As I thrilled in the new challenges, I transmitted the sheer and utter enjoyment that I got out of it. People, in turn, began to give me new challenges. I received my first invitation to teach abroad - in another language! I accepted it and the folks helped me stumble through my Spanish. (I already spoke Portuguese.) They were patient with me since they felt that I really had something to contribute. Years later, many of those patient students became the founding members of the first Psychodrama Association in Ecuador.

I was sent to Nicaragua in January, 1989. My heart broke over the suffering the war and the tornadoes had wrought. I shed many tears with the mothers whose sons had been lost in the civil war. I was humbled by the prayers that blessed the food we ate. Truly these were holy meals. These people prayed gratefully, some of them absolutely certain that they did not know where their next meal was coming from, thankful that they had this one. I fell in love with them, and in the geography of my heart, you will find a special place for the "Nicas".

Ironically, I discovered I was especially equipped to teach emotional recovery. I had come through. I knew it could be done.

The other children I never had have become new endeavors. I went into the "reproduction mode" by writing books and articles, slowly at first, later with more confidence. I "gave birth" to new lives in the consulting room. I understood that I saw it happen because I believed they could do it. And I believed because spring had at last come knocking on my door.

In the beginning of the convalescence period, I was constantly thinking of when I would remarry, how this would happen. Each new person (read: the males of the human species) that came into my life was eyed as a potential Prince Charming. As I recovered I saw it for what it was: pure foolishness. I could not depend on the existence of another person in my life to bring me fulfillment. What if Prince Charming never arrived and I spent a lifetime, treading water, waiting for "Mr. Godot"? Once this was settled, I could be friends with everyone. In truth, as time went on and my life got more exciting, I doubted that a relationship could enrich my life even more. I remained open to it (avoiding the familiar trap that "men are all alike - none of them are worthy to be trusted"), but I quit chasing it down. That was a big step.

I remembered that God had called me into the ministry of reconciliation when I was seventeen. God is faithful and had brought that ministry into fruition in these years since my divorce. Life has never been better. As a matter of fact, I could never have imagined that it could be this good without marriage. I have had the chance to travel throughout Latin America and learn a new language. I have new friends who have different habits and customs. I have been ushered into the heartfelt intimacy of the people who populate my continent. What a privilege! I have been loved, appreciated and recognized through my efforts. (I have also been criticized and had a few rocks thrown at me, but I discovered that I can take that, too.) Better yet, I have learned to love others better and to comprehend a new dimension of the mercy of God.

My daughter and I are closer than we have ever been now that sorrow no longer silences us. There is no shame to being a reorganized family - just "differentness". God is ever-present in our lives. We turn to God because there is now a relationship of deep-felt trust. Having faced so many other difficult moments in the past, when the invitation to move to Ecuador came through, she took up the challenge with me. Why not? We had overcome even tougher hurdles together.

My relationship with God has deepened and the trust has reached a new level. Things don't have to go my way for me to maintain my friendship with God.

Finally, I have perceived that the Apostle Paul was right - when we are weak, then we are strong. Out of my greatest weaknesses and anguish have come my greatest blessings and strengths. Or as Ernest Hemingway once put it, "life breaks us all... but some of us become strong in the broken places." God has made me strong in my broken places.

*(Originally published in **Single Women: Affirming our Spiritual Journeys** (EUA:Bergin & Garvey, 1993).*

Separation and Divorce

Many years ago I attended some presentations in Quito, Ecuador, by Dr. Jorge Maldonado, on the Family Cycle. As he developed the topics each night, I realized that there was a situation he had not mentioned and that affected our families, Christian or not: divorce. To remedy this, I put some thoughts to paper and included the emotional tasks, the conflicts and the healing aspects of the process of emotional recovery after divorce.

I personally believe that divorce is like an abortion: it interrupts the natural developmental process of family life. A separation implies many immediate losses which have to be grieved and other recovery tasks; but it can also mean some benefits, although these tend to show up in the long haul.

Grieving the losses

The first thing those touched by divorce must face are the losses. The family loses the living arrangements wherein all of its members spent time under the same roof. Sometimes this loss can be a relief, if living together had turned into a nightmare. But even in the worst of situations, people lose others with whom they were used to living. There is a definite shift in who lives with whom.

There are explanations to give: why doesn't my father live here anymore? Why did you stop loving each other? When is he coming back? How come you two can't stay together? Why doesn't my mother want to live with you anymore? And so on... These are very pertinent questions that deserve honest replies, but that are very difficult to answer because many times even the people involved don't really know all the *whys*.

It is not just the children who go through these changes but the adults also lose each other. People get married to stay together, and a divorce ends this life project. The dream of having someone with whom to share a life or to count on when times get rough, someone to lean on during difficult times or share the joy, have children and age together... this dream with this person is over.

Other things also come to an end. Often the family has to move because the economic situation doesn't allow them to stay where they are. The salaries that once supported one family now have to support two households. If mom didn't work outside the home before, she certainly will now! This means that the children lose both parents in one sense. If the mother works outside the home for eight hours and then has to come home and solve at least another hundred million problems she does not have the time and attention to invest in the children as she did before. Many household tasks that had been shared now weigh on only one spouse, especially if the children aren't old enough to help yet.

The couple who separates lose their civil status. This seems pretty obvious, but the consequences are more subtle. It is expected, especially in Latin cultures where I come from, that men will start going out with other women. If the woman starts dating other men, her reputation often suffers. She is now a "divorced" woman, and has lost, in a certain sense, the "virtuous" protection that marriage afforded her.

Oftentimes the proper names of the spouses are also lost in the shuffle. The man becomes the "father of the children"; the woman is the "mother of the kids", as if to emphasize that what now keeps these two connected is no longer the love they vowed, but the children they had. If it weren't for the children, perhaps they would never again see the person whom they promised to love and cherish forever.

Reorganizing life:
Thus begins the second emotional task: that of reorganizing and adjusting to changes. The schedules have to be reorganized as well as money, and time. What do you do when you come home and there is no one waiting for you? How do you count the days until you can see the children again? What do you do with empty weekends? What about invitations to go out? What if the guy wants to have sex? Or what if I *don't* want to have sex with her?

This is a period of many difficult questions and no easy answers. It's like being a five-year-old and having to learn life all over again. And in the midst of it all is an overwhelming depression that often threatens to take over.

Time is the greatest ally. Slowly, you can learn to get to know yourself better, in a new way. On your own, it is possible to find out what you are really like and what you can really do. It's nice to realize that your own company is pleasant. And it's really nice to have time to do some things by and for yourself, like reading a book, or listening to music, or an unexpected outing, or just think about the mundane and as well as the existential things of life. It is really great to discover that being alone is neither a punishment nor a curse. It can be a great blessing if done well.

How to relate to the children is another topic of reorganization. What is it going to be like from now on? No one can be mother *and* father, even if you try to do the things that pertain to both roles. A mother who does "daddy things" is still a mother because she is a woman. It is important to redefine these relationships and what they will look like from now on. And if the father leaves the picture completely, it will be especially important to find other healthy men that can fill that role, like grandparents, or uncles or church friends. Men play a really important role in confirming gender/sexual identity, so "adoptive" fathers are key to navigating these waters.

Another aspect of reorganization has to do with the issue of romance and affection. When do you start dating, or do you do it all? It is common, at some point, for a new person to arrive on the scene. There is not a simple answer to a lot of these delicate issues, but it is a wonderful feeling to "fall in love" again and realize that you are capable of a whole range of feelings that once seemed totally dead. Trying to deal with this and the children can be dicey. Most children have trouble seeing a parent with someone else in a romantic way. Thinking it through beforehand is probably a wise move, for it is something that will eventually come up. A good rule of thumb is to not introduce them to the kids unless it is really getting serious. For children to have to watch a parade of boyfriends or girlfriends is not conducive to a respectful relationship with the parent, and is quite unsettling for the kids.

Conflicts

The children need to understand that they are not at fault for the divorce. It is very easy for the kids to take on this guilt trip for the most unusual and often strange reasons. They need to be told, verbally and frequently, that this was an adult decision, made by adults and that unfortunately they are stuck with the consequences of it.

Some of these decisions bring on enormous conflicts which is unfortunately normal to some extent. If we could only realize how ambivalent everyone is feeling in all of these relationships, it might make it easier to resolve the conflicts in a healthier manner.

Ambivalence is a defining word for this period and often ignored by those involved. How can you be so angry at someone with whom you had fallen so deeply in love? How can you still love someone who has hurt you so badly?

As in any situation of loss, good things are also lost, even if they presently have less weight. There was a time of sharing that was enjoyable. It seems that to admit this when there is a divorce is a betrayal of the separation decision or admitting that you still love the other person. But the truth is that a relationship that took so much time to build up cannot end in a day. The opposite of love is not hate, but indifference. It takes a long time to get to the point where what the other spouse is doing doesn't affect you anymore. This is normal.

A divorce changes the direction of emotional investment in the relationship. When you get married, you do it so you can be closer, spend more time together and have greater intimacy. A divorce inverts the direction of this movement. Now there is a greater distancing from each other, an intentional loss of intimacy. In the same way that it took time and effort to forge that intimacy, it takes time and effort to lose it.

A common defense mechanism often comes into play in these situations as well. There is a tendency to badmouth or belittle the other's image in an attempt to convince yourself that the loss is all about losing something or someone who is unworthy. It is much easier to think that I am losing something that is bad, than to admit the real size of the loss. Good things have also been lost and that can be hard to accept although very necessary.

Children also are ambivalent towards their parents. The adults are supposed to provide support, protection, love and security to the children. They should offer a marital situation wherein the children's basic needs are provided and where they can develop into emotionally healthy adults. With a divorce, the parents become the source of *suffering* not consolation. Children acknowledge they desperately need their parents because they fear they can't survive without them. But oftentimes they are angry at the "betrayal" of their parents: why should they have to "pay" for their parent's problems? These issues are not always talked about clearly. Usually, they just turn into feelings, but they are present. Children often feel their parents are the guilty ones, but are afraid to admit it, even to themselves, especially since they depend so heavily on them.

Problem areas:

When the children ally themselves with one parent. Whether this comes from the child or the parent, everyone loses. When a relationship ends, one of the spouses is not completely right and the other completely wrong, although both will often go to great lengths to prove that the other is wrong. Perhaps one of the spouses has given up on the relationship and the commitment that was made at marriage, and no longer wants to continue to invest in making the marriage work. Children are not objective observers of family break-ups. They have a stake in what is happening.

It is also unfair to ask them to take sides. When parents insinuate, "if you go with him/her, then it's because you don't love me anymore"… the children are in a terrible bind. Of course they have never quit loving either of their parents just because there is a divorce. Plus, the children want to be loyal to both of them, but quickly realize that the parents are getting on opposite teams of the playing field. It gets really hard when the children perceive that when they please one parent, they displease the other. Sometimes they choose to live with only one parent in order not to have to deal with this constant strain and stress. However, most children who opt out of a relationship with one parent eventually regret it (except in those cases where the parent is a physical/sexual danger to the child's well-being).

A divorce should not be construed as armed warfare. People shouldn't have to take sides. The parents are separating, but the children are not divorcing them. It is really hard for the children to have to live with the consequences of the decisions of their parents.

Using the children against the other spouse. Since children are so important to both parents, to deprive one of them of seeing each other is a very powerful weapon. Once again, the losers are the children. They begin to see that they are often being used as a piece on an enormous chessboard of life. Children have feelings, too. Do not use your children as weapons!

Remarry quickly after a divorce. This is not a good way to go at getting over a divorce. Obviously, for some people, this was the whole reason for the divorce, but in those situations where it was not, this is not a healthy way to recover from a divorce. There isn't enough time to grieve the loss of the previous relationship. The other aspect of this trap is that it is an attempt to numb the pain of separation. The issue is that the pain should be worked through and not avoided. If grief is not properly dealt with, it comes back in other, more hurtful ways in the future.

Others marry quickly so as not to "burn" or get caught up in a promiscuous lifestyle. This was never a good motivation for marriage. Once the fire burns out, many regret their decision, and divorce once again.

Others have questions about their own sexuality, especially after a divorce. Some wonder if the sexual issue was part of the reason for the divorce. Maybe I wasn't "man enough" for her? Maybe I couldn't keep him happy in bed? Some try some sexual experimentation outside the Biblical grounds for sex in an attempt to find out if the problem was "me or him?" Since sex was established by God for a lasting marriage covenant, this "dabbling" with sex will also reap painful results.

"Free sexual life". There are some people who will go into a promiscuous lifestyle after a divorce, ironically enough, as an attempt to stave off intimate relationships. It seems rather paradoxal that what God created to be the most intimate form of expression between a man and a woman can be used for exactly the opposite purpose. But we see a lot of this happening. A repetitive cycle of "one-night stands" keeps a person from ever

getting emotionally intimate with anyone. It keeps them at a "safe" emotional distance. The reasoning is that "if I don't get into a committed loving relationship, then I will never again risk the pain of divorce". This way, the person thinks they will never get hurt... nor will they ever be happy either.

What can be done to help in these situations?

Obviously, the ideal thing is to strengthen the marriage bond in such a way that divorces never happen. There are many groups that are committed to marriage retreats and building up a couple's skills in such a way as to avoid divorces. However, the fact of life is that divorces are occurring with ever growing frequency. So what's to be done?

One of the first suggestions is *to live intensely what is part of the grief process.* This is the road to emotional recovery. The Bible tells us that we should not think it strange when suffering finds us, but rather rejoice in it (I Pe. 4:12-13). Moffat's translation says that we should "embrace suffering" since it develops our character. We are not to do this in that medieval way of flagellation, but live out our pain, knowing that it will end, and God will bring good out of the pain. It takes courage to let yourself hurt, but it will come to an end and the scars will be marks of victory, of one who has overcome and is on the road to emotional health.

Give yourself time. There are very few situations where time resolves things, but grief is one of the few where time is on your side. Don't imagine that you can do the same things you were able to do before. You don't have that much emotional energy right now. Sometimes, well-meaning friends or relatives will say that it's time to move on, but emotional recovery is a long process, and it usually takes 1-2 years to really begin to get over it. Be patient with yourself. There will be better days and worse days, but slowly the better days will outnumber the others.

Don't worry about relapse. Sometimes, after you've spent a really good few days or weeks, something will jump out and bring up all sorts of memories or desires. This is also normal. Be depressed for a little while, but don't cave in forever. Feel the pain and let it go its way. Eventually, it will go away.

Finally, a divorce can be *an experience of growth*. It is not one of the most pleasant ways of maturing, but once the separation is inevitable, it can be used *for* you instead of against you. Suffering is not the end of the world, although no one enjoys it. Jesus learned obedience from the things he suffered (Heb. 5:8) and he assured us that in this world we would have trouble (John 15:8). It is better to see suffering as an instrument that builds character and obedience than to rebel against something that is pretty inevitable in this lifetime. All of us suffer in one way or another. A divorce can be the great crisis that pushes us in a new direction, opening new horizons and giving us the chance to conquer new things in life.

The Pain of Divorce

13 "Good," said David. "I will make an agreement with you. But I demand one thing of you: Do not come into my presence unless you bring Michal daughter of Saul when you come to see me." 14 Then David sent messengers to Ish-Bosheth son of Saul, demanding, "Give me my wife Michal, whom I betrothed to myself for the price of a hundred Philistine foreskins."2 Samuel 3:13-16 (NIV)

15 So Ish-Bosheth gave orders and had her taken away from her husband Paltiel son of Laish. 16 Her husband, however, went with her, weeping behind her all the way to Bahurim. Then Abner said to him, "Go back home!" So he went back.

One of the most obvious aspects of a divorce is that it hurts, and it hurts a lot. It hurts so much that some people will do anything to avoid the pain. There is no such thing as a painless divorce, as we can see from the passage about Paltiel, mourning the loss of his wife.

The pain of separation and divorce is enormous. It seems like it will never end, that you will never be able to wake up in the morning and hear the birds sing or enjoy the sunshine or see the blue sky. This is normal. It takes months, sometimes years for a person to digest such a great loss. It is one of the greatest losses in life, since it ends one of the most important life projects: a marriage. Oftentimes, this pain comes accompanied by a feeling of failure because such an important part of our lives has come to an end.

It doesn't matter if the decision was one-sided or by common agreement. The pain is still there. Learning to live together took time and learning to live apart will, too. Oftentimes, people will accuse others of still loving their mate because they are still mourning the loss. Is it really love? Hard to tell, but the truth is that no one can get over a relationship that was so important in a short amount of time. It takes time to become indifferent to each other.

Avoiding the pain is the worst attitude possible. It turns up as symptoms of physical pain (psychosomatic illnesses), or behavioral disorders or other unhealthy ways of expressing the pain. The Bible tells us that there is a time to mourn (Ecc. 3). Don't short-circuit the process or you will shortchange yourself. It is also important to explain to those around you that mourning is important. People will try to cheer you up by saying that it's not that bad. It is *really that* bad. Let people cry and mourn. When a person dies, there is a funeral. When a marriage dies, we still need to mourn the relationship that is gone.

A marriage relationship is dying. Even though parents are their children's parents "until death do us part", the intimate relationship that once existed in a marriage bond has to be undone. From being the most intimate person in my life (that sense of "oneness"), the spouse needs to become a stranger, with whom I no longer share my daily life. At some point, the only topic of conversation left will be about the children.

Seek comfort. It will hurt for a while, but it will not hurt forever. A loss properly grieved will not leave lasting scars. It will give you strength, maturity, wisdom, and compassion for others. Someone who is going through a divorce right now will not believe these words, but it's true. The day will come when you can talk about your ex-spouse without trembling or crying or fear, anger or desolation. If you dive deeply into the pain of divorce you will surface a stronger and wiser person. You will know that suffering hurts, but it doesn't kill.

A well-grieved loss brings emotional gains and benefits. The big danger is denial, trying to "be strong" in order to not feel the pain. Since it will eventually go away, why not go ahead and grieve it through? Buried pain never dies. A loss that is not properly grieved will last much longer, and sometimes forever. It may require professional services later on in order to solve the problem. There is no shame in hurting. Parents don't like to see their children suffer, but they can set the example for them. As parents allow themselves to grieve, to cry in front of their children and admit their own pain, they allow their children to hurt and cry together. This will go a long way in teaching them how to deal with grief.

The most important thing to remember is that God also consoles us. He is the Father of all comfort and mercy. He will come running to meet you on the road of recovery. He is always waiting for you with open arms and a warm heart.

Suggestions for when the pain gets really bad

1. Let it out in healthy ways. It will go away some day. Write a letter that you will never send and burn it. Start a journal. "Kill" some pillows on your bed, swatting it when no one is looking. Talk to an empty chair or to a favorite tree.
2. Reflect on what is happening to you. Perhaps you can participate in a support group for others who are going through similar experiences. A support group will give you comfort, understanding, and a safe place to bounce off your thoughts and feelings. If there are none around you, think about starting one. There are plenty of hurting people around going through divorces.
3. Consider psychotherapy or counseling with someone you trust. It can help you understand what happened and what is happening now. It can help you understand how you got into the relationship you did, and how to make a better choices.
4. Don't leave the church. The brothers and sisters should be able to help you through this difficult phase. Ask God to help you find people who will lend you their ears. Usually the pastor is too busy to accompany someone going through a divorce, but there are other brothers and sisters that can help if they only know how bad you're hurting.

Helping others who are hurting

1. *Listen.* When you have finished listening, listen some more. Listening is really *really* important.
2. *Listen without judgment.* Don't try to figure out who is right or wrong. Every story has at least two sides to it. Don't try to figure out if the separation should or shouldn't have occurred. That's their problem. The person who is hurting needs a friendly shoulder, not advice.
3. Remember that people who are going through a divorce can be rather boring and tiresome. All they know how to talk about is their divorce. Try to do things together, take them out, or invite them to your house. *"Adopt" them.* But don't insist. Take their kids out if they need some "alone" time. Invite them for Sunday dinner which is usually hard time for

families; or Christmas or vacations. Let them know they can say no, but that they are welcome. Going the second mile is a lot of work, but that's what the good news is all about.

Her Lamp Does Not Go Out at Night

"Mommy! Mommy! I'm scared! I dreamt there was a snake and it was going to get me. Now I can't sleep anymore! I can still see it whenever I shut my eyes..."

Raquel crawled into my bed, and stuck her trembling little self under my covers. I hugged the young child and spoke to her softly, sighing on the inside over one more sleep interruption. But that's how children are... sleeping through the night was a luxury for youth, not for moms.

"Mommy, I want to pray. That way I can quit trembling."

I prayed with Raquel, asking the Lord to take away her fear and that He would give her tranquil sleep. I had barely said amen, when she launched out into her own prayer, so pure, so simple. When she finished, she turned and said to me:

"I can still remember the snake, and I can go back to sleep without being afraid. Please stay close to me until I fall asleep again."

As I held on to her hand, she turned and fell asleep in my arms in a matter of moments. I was amazed at her simplicity and how quickly she resolved her crisis. But, after all, this was what I had taught her, that the Lord was the "father of our household" and that we depended on Him for the solution of our problems.

As I reflected on it, this had been one of the greatest gains of my separation: being able to raise my daughter in the ways of the Lord. We were a family: God was the Husband, the Father, and we would lean on Him whenever we had our troubles. It was under His wings that we sought refuge and shade.

While my daughter was sleeping in my arms, I laid there for a long time thinking things over. I came to the conclusion that whoever invented the double bed never had a clue how much he had helped mothers. In a few minutes, I would take Raquel back to her bed, where she always slept. But it was so comfortable to have a bed where both of us fit, with our dreams and our prayers.

Sometimes, I would fall asleep before I took her back to her bed. In the morning she would look at me with that mischievous little face, and a twinkle in her eye, and say:

"I slept here all night, didn't I?"
"Yes, you did, but this isn't your bed."
"I know, but I was so scared that I came here..!"
"Yeah, but don't get used to it," feigning anger.

I well knew that the scene would repeat itself. But the important thing was that my daughter knew where to find me when she needed me.

The important thing was that my lamp did not go out at night.

Life Goes On...

Dear friend:

You want to know if there is life after divorce...?

A few days ago I got a phone call from Brazil, telling me about three pastors that died in a car accident. One of them was my dearest uncle; the other a missionary who had consecrated my daughter when she was born; the third was a good friend of my mother's. The fourth person had been late and the three had left without him. He cried inconsolably at the funeral.

So I've spent the last few days thinking about my aunt and the other widows. I've been accompanying three widowed people here in Quito during this last year as well, people who are going through that difficult mourning phase that leads to emotional recovery. Obviously, their pain reminds me of what I went through with my divorce. Who knows, as I answer your question, perhaps I'm writing a little to all of these widowed people and thinking a bit about what the future will bring them.

Does life go on? Yes, but sometimes we almost wish it didn't. The pain of separation by death or divorce is so great that we often ask ourselves how we are going to survive so much emotional hurt. During the first moments, days and weeks, it's hard to imagine that life could ever go on at all. Many people feel this way. They think it would be better to die in order to not feel the pain. Sometimes, waking up in the morning is like awakening to the nightmare of life because it makes us face reality as it is now. This depression can last some time, sometimes a year or more.

Some people really can't stand to see others suffer and want them to get it over with quickly. As a result, they try to console us with empty words. The friendship and support of our family and friends is always welcome, but the lack of permission to hurt can be very uncomfortable. This is a time of mourning. People need to cry, let it out, and forget about "being strong". You are going through the loss of a great love, or a dream that did not come true, or perhaps even a really bad relationship that ended. It is necessary to cry until the tears finally run out.

Time will make it better. When we have good friends that help us through this period, it gets easier. A good friend is someone who lets us talk about the death of the loved one, or the marriage that ended. Talking about it helps. A few days ago, a young fellow told me about the attitude of some friends on the anniversary of his mother's death: "It's talking about my mother bothers them. I don't get it. She's died, but I don't want to forget her. She taught me many good things." So we had a cup of coffee together and he told me about his mother. What he now has of her are the memories.

You know something, my friend? In the beginning, even remembering hurts. Yesterday, I went to look for a document I had put away and found articles written by my uncle. The tears came hot and fast. That's the way it was when my marriage broke up. I would traipse across things that would remind me of him. It was like these things said, "See? He's not coming back. The separation is definitive and final." Even though I had already reached a point where I did not want reconciliation, it hurt to know that such an important life project had failed. Those who lose their spouses to death must hurt even more!

But, yes, life goes on. One day, you will wake up and the sky will not be gray. One day you'll ask yourself, will I ever be happy again? How can I be happy if my spouse has died? How can life be happy if my marriage failed? Guilt can be subtle and piercing, like a serpent. This guilt trip, which is false guilt, will often try to sabotage the fragile joy that begins to bloom at certain times.

This mourning period is a time to pull back. A widower I know turned in his managerial position after fifteen years because he didn't want the responsibility of dealing with the office problems after the death of his wife. He needed time for himself. A year later, the energy is coming back. He has gone through his mourning in a wise manner. He respected his emotional and physical boundaries. Later, he told me that every day at 3 in the afternoon, he would go home to be alone, and cry. It had been a year of emotional convalescence.

So... what can we do to handle this in a constructive manner?

Do what you can. Don't expect too much out of yourself. There are things we *have* to do: the children have to eat, clothes have to get washed, and the salary has to come in. Do the minimum you can for a while. Convalescing takes a lot of energy and strength and that's why doctors tell us we have to get off our feet when we break a leg. We also need to rest when it is our heart that has been broken.

Don't let people pressure you. Many folks think that after three months, you should be over this. Based on my own experience, recovery takes time. I remember that many of the divorcees and widows I talked to in my practice would complain that their friends and family didn't understand them. Oftentimes it was only after three months, that they really began to believe in their heart of hearts that their spouse would never come back. In the beginning, it's like the person was just traveling. Unconsciously, we await their return. It is only as day after day after day goes by that we realize that they are really not going to come back ever and we have to begin a new phase of emotional recovery.

Don't get upset about relapses. They are normal. Six years after my divorce, I woke up to a miserable day. I couldn't figure it out until I realized at work that it would have been a wedding anniversary. The next day, I was fine again. The heart heals, but the scar remains.

We have the privilege of having happiness return to our lives at some point. Perhaps it will be a different kind of happiness, because the hand of God has sustained us with his comfort. How many times did I climb into the Lord's lap and ask for his embrace? Like the Apostle Paul, we carry in our bodies and in our hearts the marks of our suffering, that quiet knowledge and the memory of whom we have lost. One day we will be able to wake up and not cry. One day we *will* get over it.

Ten years after having lost my grandfather, Grandma told me that every morning she greeted his photograph in her bedroom. The difference was that now she could do it without crying, but trusting that one day she would see him again. But for right now, life went on.

Hang in there, my friend. Yes, life does go on.

Love, Esly

And When You Miss Him...?

Don't worry about it and don't make a big deal out of it. Missing a significant person in your life is natural and normal.

A marriage is made up of many things and many emotions. There is love, friendship, intimacy, and a thousand other feelings. When a marriage ends there are even more different feelings that come up. These are perhaps more complicated, more complex. There isn't just *one* feeling. Since there weren't just bad things in the relationship, when a separation occurs it doesn't mean that all of the good things never existed. Even when we know that the relationship had to end it is important to acknowledge that good things were present as well. After all, we got married because we believed that it would work and we wanted to live together for the rest of our lives.

When we miss the other person it is because an intimate relationship does not end in 24 hours. Like I said earlier, a separation means we have to change directions, from intimacy to estrangement. When we got married, we learned what the other person was like, how they did things, and what pleased them: He likes less salt in his food; she hates a wet towel on the bed. Sometimes we get to know each other so well that we can tell what kind of a mood they are in just by their footsteps. We share very significant experiences, like having children together. Seeing that child come out of our inner parts as if from nowhere is one of the most bonding experiences there is on the face of the earth. When relatives died, we cried on the spouse's shoulder. When a child got sick, it was our spouse who helped us care for them. So we see that it was even (or perhaps *because* of) the difficult circumstances that brought us together as we faced crises and got through them.

So when a divorce happens, this whole process of growing in intimacy comes to a grinding halt and has to go into reverse. So from intimate, the other has to become a stranger. This process takes time, sometimes years.

Does missing the other mean that you are still in love with them? I don't know. There are so many feelings involved. The Bible says that when we marry we become one flesh. Divorce means ripping apart this one flesh into two different parts, so you can imagine why it hurts so deeply.

I once heard Joe Dallas say that "we should never underestimate the power of the familiar." Brilliant. It is incredible how we continue to do and say things just because they are familiar to us. We miss familiar ways of life, routine, things we shared and did together. We knew what was expected of us, good or bad (or ugly).

I've often seen this with battered women who remain in a relationship they know needs to end for their own safety and that of their children. But the unknown looms ahead with such terror that familiarity often wins out. They know what to expect, even if it is a black eye.

So we miss the other person when there is a divorce because we also miss what is familiar, what is expected. A separation imposes a slew of new challenges, some of which we welcome and others that we have to face regardless. This is normal. It is normal to fear the unknown and be afraid that you won't be able to handle it. We have faced these fears since the day we left our mother's womb. We continue to seek that Eden where we can rest and live eternally in familiar circumstances, but unfortunately, we will not find that in this life.

But don't despair. If the divorce is inevitable, tell your heart to hang in there. Things will eventually get better. Give time its opportunity to do its work. When you miss the other it doesn't necessarily mean you still love them. It is a sign that you are still linked in some way to the familiar things in the relationship. Perhaps if we can understand that, it makes it easier to deal with the nostalgia. If we don't feed it, it will go away. Be aware that there may be relapses, but they are part of a process and not the whole picture. Grief is an up-and-down process.

Our emotions do not always keep up with our decisions. Sometimes we have the conviction that this is the best decision, but our hearts are not cooperative. It takes time for love to die. Sometimes our marriages are crucified by divorce, but it takes time for it to finally pass away.

My Son Is Getting a Divorce...

I had only one son, whom my husband and I tried to raise with love and care. He grew up like any other normal child, went to Sunday school and church. We raised him in the Biblical truth of God that is so fundamental to our own lives. He went to college, got a degree and started dating the woman he eventually married. The wedding was beautiful and the pastor who officiated was the same one who had married my husband and me. They had two children that are our pride and joy! The couple had their ups and downs which we figured were pretty normal, but after six years of marriage, they have been fighting so much lately that they have decided to separate. My son is going through a divorce! And now, what do I do?

- A sad and worried mother

A divorce is something very difficult for the children involved as well as for those who are accompanying the process and suffer its consequences. Many times, there are enormous conflicts involving the children... who are your grandchildren.

The Biblical example that comes to mind comes from the book of Ruth and has to do with Naomi. I have asked myself many times what kind of a mother-in-law was this woman that her daughter-in-law was willing to follow? Ruth left her family, her home, the land she was familiar with, friends and even her own customs in order to go to a foreign and unknown land, compelled by the life and example of Naomi, and their relationship. I have often asked the Lord for Naomi's wisdom and that I might become a mother-in-law like her!

I am going to give free rein to my imagination for a few moments and share a few things that I think Naomi might tell us if she had to face a situation like yours. Even though the book of Ruth does not deal directly with separation and divorce, I think there are a few things we can learn from her example.

First of all, we must take into consideration *that no one changes anyone.* I don't think Naomi tried to change Ruth. At the beginning of the story, this Israelite mother-in-law encouraged her daughter-in-law to stay in Moab and return to her family and Moabite customs. Naomi accepted Ruth as she was: a Moabitess.

Naomi could see in Ruth a woman of integrity that had been a good wife to her son, now deceased. Surely part of the reason that Ruth followed after Naomi was due to Naomi's unconditional acceptance. Naomi had respected their married life, and now that she was widowed, Ruth knew that she could still continue to trust her mother-in-law.

So, please be aware that your opinion will not change what has happened. We are often tempted to give our children advice about what is going on. In the same way that parents are unable to keep their children from getting married, they are equally unable to keep them from getting divorced. To the contrary, oftentimes parents contribute towards a divorce if they are unable to let their children live their lives and make their own decisions; if they are unable to allow their children to "leave mother and father" as the book of Genesis teaches us. I know a pastor who has the parents swear before God and the church during the wedding ceremony that they will not interfere in the married lives of the new couple. For some, it is very difficult to make this promise, much less keep it.

Therefore, be aware that there isn't a whole lot that can be done to change the situation. What you can do is accept this fact. Acceptance does not imply approval. We do not always approve of what our children do, but we need to have the maturity to accept and respect their decisions, even when it hurts us.

Accepting the situation will give you permission to grieve. After all, they are not the only ones who are suffering losses due to the separation. You may also be losing the chance to be able to spend time with someone you really liked. Sometimes it gets worse and the visits to grandchildren become very limited. These are all losses that need to be felt and grieved, and are often very painful. But it is better to be able to face this pain and get through it than have to drink from the chalice of resentment later on.

This is a time when our children need to be heard and understood. However, most people are tempted to do exactly the opposite: give advice. It is hard to listen to their pain, but it is very important that your son understand that whatever decision they take, that he can still count on you. Oftentimes, our children would rather talk to their friends, and that's fine. But they need to know that they can count on you.

One of the most disastrous and common mistakes is to take sides. Don't do this!! Everyone loses. Every marriage story has two sides to it and so does every separation. The Bible teaches us the path of love. This is a moment when love is needed most. Be like Naomi: behave in such a way that someone will want to follow your example.

Remember the children. They are the ones who suffer the most in all of this, and none of it is their fault. They can also be the ones who recover most quickly if you can help them along the way. If you take sides, or speak badly about one of their parents, they will not feel comfortable about sharing confidences with you. Your grandchildren don't want you to agree or disagree with their complaints or the enormous pain they feel. They just need someone who will listen and comfort. They need affection even when they are acting with hostility and rebellion. There is very little that love, affection and good boundaries won't cure.

Finally, *remember to pray* for all of those involved in this situation, including yourself, for the "prayer of the just availeth much". You don't necessarily have to pray for their reconciliation although that is a legitimate issue and we can bring it before the Lord, since oftentimes that is the desire of our heart. But the final decision will belong to the couple. Sometimes, people are so engrossed in bringing about a reconciliation that they don't take other issues into consideration. Pray and ask for comfort from heaven, and that the Father of all mercy and consolation may comfort all of those involved in these difficult times. It is impossible to accompany the suffering of others without hurting, too, especially when it is a son. Grieve the loss and do not be ashamed of it. But receive the comfort of God for these difficulties. The Lord teaches us that He comforts us in our pain so that we can comfort others with the same comfort He has given us. (2. Cor. 1:3:7). May it be so for all of us!

Who Gets to Keep the Friends?

First of all, it depends on whose friends they were. When we get married, we have friends that are "mine", "yours", and "ours". "My" friends usually stay with me. Why would they go away? Usually these are the friends that see us through thick and then. (They are the ones that take sides... *my* side!)

The ex-spouse's friends usually take his side. Friendship requires this kind of loyalty. Friends take sides, and his are his and mine are mine.

The interesting situations come up when the friends belonged to both of us. Some take sides and that settles the boundary issues, but others decide they want to be friends with both of you, and that is where the challenge arises.

I clearly remember some friends who had some brilliant solutions. Soon after my legal separation, Marcia called up:

"Esly, it is my husband's birthday and I would like for you to come to the party on Saturday night."

I decided the issue was too touchy to talk about over the phone, so I went over to her house.

"Did you invite him?" I asked.

"Who... So-and so, your ex-husband?"

"Yes."

I took a deep breath, and thought it over for a few moments and then I told her, "Then I'm not coming. Or rather, I will come another day to greet your husband for his birthday, but I really don't want to see So-and-so, especially since I know that he will probably show up accompanied by someone else. I'm just not healed enough for it yet."

She was saddened, but she understood. A few days later, I went over to pay the call I had promised, and she said:

"Esly, I know how we can solve this problem. We want to be friends with both of you, and we understand each one's side of the story, and we are not going to take sides. So we have decided that we will take turns inviting each of you to our parties. We will be careful not to invite both of you to the same one. What do you think?"

I thought it was great. And that's how things worked out. For years, I was invited to their parties and I had a lot of fun. I knew I could accept their invitation without having to worry about it. Sometimes I heard about some party to which I had not been invited, and I understood that it was the other's turn to get invited. I felt respected and protected. It was a fantastic solution. When I remarried, they were amongst the friends who came to my wedding.

Not all friends are so wise, but this is an example of a solution that was good for everyone. Those involved in these situations need discernment, but friendships need to be based on maturity, respect and love.

On the other hand, there are other friends we lose along the way. Interests change, as well as priorities, rhythm and time constraints. Sometimes our lifestyles change. Some we are sorry to lose and others are gone without our really ever having perceived it. Others we lose because they reject us. That is very sad. I've seen even brothers and sisters in Christ do this to each other. This is a time when we really need to hang together with our friends. We especially need friends who will accompany us in prayer. It is not up to others to judge the reasons for our separation, but to accompany us and ask for the wisdom of God for our friendship.

Finally, for those who do not have this problem because they have no friends, I give a word of warning! I once heard a friend say, "I can live without a husband, but I cannot live without my friends." Good friends are a special gift from God. Some are "closer than a brother". To have good friends it is imperative to be a good friend. We need to be committed to this art. Sometimes our friends are our substitute family when we do not have family members around, or family just doesn't understand. Friendships are an essential part of life. We cannot live without them. The lack of friends implies a lack of emotional health. We are social beings by divine design. "It is not good for man to be alone". It is not good to be without friends, and the family of faith must set the example.

Divorced, Yet Friends: Is this really possible?

"Well, we could at least be friends..."

I looked at the phone and thought, "Us? Friends?" It seemed that the last thing I would want at that point was for us to be friends...!

One of the things that is often given up after a divorce is friendship. Many times, a true friendship was never there (or they would still be married.) Other times, the break-up was so bitter, that a friendship is unimaginable. Other times, distance and discretion are the better part of valor.

But there are others who would truly like to be friends, and it is worth examining the issue.

My mom, Dona Zizi, always quoted an old Brazilian proverb, "You can't have all the good things of life in only one sack." It was her understanding of "you really can't have it all". Some people want to lose the marriage, but not the relationship and that is not always possible. Of course there were good things in the relationship or people wouldn't have gotten married, but it is not always possible to be friends.

What motivates this kind of request? Sometimes, people are reluctant to admit how much it hurts to end a marriage, and they don't want to get in contact with the deep grief that is involved. Maintaining a friendship helps to maintain the illusion that all is well. Others are sincere in their desire to be able to maintain some kind of friendship, but more often than not, it too falls into the ambivalent feelings that surround most divorces. There were bad things in the marriage, but there were good things, too.

This ambivalence is normal. After all, as we invert the movement of the relationship, transforming that intimate person into a stranger, we also begin to lose the routine of daily life. One more loss to digest... or to try to avoid.

When we think about being friends, perhaps it is important to ask ourselves what friends are like. What does it mean to be a friend? What is it we do with them? Friends are people we trust. They accept us as we are and like us, warts and all. We respect each other. We go over to each other's house. Now then, do you really want your "ex" to come calling at your house? We share our dreams and desires with our friends, what we are struggling with and where we want to go with our lives. We expect loyalty, faithfulness and trust from there... do you get the drift?

More often than not, these traits no longer exist with our ex-spouse. If we had those things in common with them we would probably still be married to them!! Divorces look more like battlefields than meadows. It never ceases to amaze me how relationships can go so sour so fast like with a divorce. Like enemies or rivals, the players are not on the same team. (Unfortunately, it would be really good if the spouses could be on the same page at least as far as the children are concerned.)

The same reasons that led to the divorce usually still exist after the divorce. Trust does not grow overnight. If they had trouble with communication issues, they probably still have them after they've signed the divorce papers. It is important to check and see if there have been any real changes in the core issues of the relationship after the divorce. Otherwise, a friendship is next to impossible.

Some people try really hard to convince the ex-spouse that they are really a good person. But if they believed that about you, the divorce probably wouldn't have happened. One of the most freeing things about a divorce is when you are finally able to let go of the idea that you have to convince the other person that you are really a great person. Once you can live with the thought that no matter what you do, they aren't going to like or accept you, you are free to be who you are and the pressure is off. You don't have to defend yourself anymore nor gain his or her approval. We can live with the idea that s/he really doesn't like me and thinks terrible things about me, and that's OK. Whatever good things evolve as a result of that is gain.

I have met some people where the relationship with the ex-spouse seems to be pretty good. This has usually happened many years after the divorce. Time has healed many wounds. A few were able to navigate the waters of their separation in a more mature fashion, and not having offended each other with "sticks, stones" and hurtful words, the relationship weathered the storm. But rarely do we see friendship in its truest form. What we often see in these cases – and would hope to see more often! – is respect. We do not have to even like other people in order to treat them with respect.

And perhaps therein lays the secret of being able to get along after a divorce; dealing respectfully, courteously with each other. This is huge, especially when children are involved. Many times, we have to "impose" respect by not allowing certain conversations to go beyond appropriate boundaries; ending discussions when it is obvious that they will no longer be fruitful at this point; watching our language and tone of voice in order to not offend unnecessarily; not taking offense easily. But all of these things are part of the discipline and exercise of the Christian virtues, and they are well worth the effort. Friendship? Perhaps not. Respect? Absolutely!

Is Reconciliation Possible?

Good question...

Let's start with those situations where I believe there is little or no chance for reconciliation. When one or both of the partners do not have a heartfelt desire to make the marriage, the likelihood of marriage survival is minimal. Marriage is a covenant between two people. When one of them breaks the contract and has no real desire to make the relationship work again, most efforts at reconciliation are pretty futile.

On the other hand, as I mentioned before, others think that a couple must stay together no matter what, and this often violates some of the basic aspects of human emotional health. There are women who will knowingly put up with their husband's infidelity and look the other way, hoping the family has more staying power. But what comes across is their disrespect for themselves and lack of self-esteem. God has never asked us to put up with marital infidelity, even though a penitent spouse and the fruit of repentance has its place. The husband begins to perceive the wife's insecurity and tends to thrive on humiliating her even further. When women put up with situations like this, what they are saying is: "I think so little of myself, I am of so little worth that I can put up with anything." This is pretty serious.

There are women who will even tolerate physical violence (besides the verbal and emotional abuse), towards themselves or their children because they do not have the courage to speak up or face new situations. "What would my life be like with out him? without a man? How would the children grow up without a father?" and the wife allows the abuse to continue until something or someone finally breaks open the family secret.

The church also has an important part to play in situations such as these. By making it clear, even from the pulpit, that such behavior is intolerable in a marriage, church leadership would crack the door for women to be able to denounce the horrors they often live in. I think some of the most unfortunate situations I have had to deal with relate to those homes where violence was present and were headed by pastors...

So this takes us to the place where we must clearly state that there are situations where reconciliation should *not* be sought unless the spouse produces long-term on-going fruit of change. Immediate intervention is a must in situations where there is risk of life, for women or children, and a therapeutic separation is necessary. Sometimes the spouse is willing to work on his behavior in order to not lose his family, but more often than not, the tendency is to deny the behavior, avoid the consequences as much as possible, and move on to the next woman who will fall in love with him and his treacherous ways.

A note about change... the highway to hell is paved with good intentions. Part of the cycle of violence are the promises to change, "to do better", "give me another chance", "it will never happen again". The only real instrument of pressure that a woman has in order to make good on her need for change is a separation. Men believe actions, not words... and so should women. They need to be willing to wait and see the changed behavior and not the spoken promise.

By separating, a woman will give her husband the possibility to consider all the losses he will incur if the relationship ends. But a separation also opens up the possibility for both to seek wise counselors who can help them on their way to recovery. If a man will not seek help for his behavior, the usual result is a divorce... which is unfortunate, but necessary to protect the family. If he does go for help, then this needs to be a mediated and therapeutic separation, where everyone gets help, from pastors or church leaders, spiritual advisors and hopefully, professionals who are experts in accompanying these situations. (We refer here to men, but these situations also happen where women are violent as well, but since the majority of cases we see have to do with men, we are referring more to the masculine case.)

This is a fairly long-term commitment. We are talking here about one to two years, and *not* one to two weeks. Certain habits take a long time to break and new habits need to be put in place. Oftentimes, there are old wounds that need to be healed in order for the behavior to change at all. Sometimes a professional medical evaluation is important to consider the possibility of medication as the process unfolds. This process is a *process*, and there must be proven fruit of change before a couple can return to living together again, and both must learn new forms of interaction with each other. This takes time.

Although in the United States the face of intervention in violent homes has changed dramatically, this is not the case in most countries of Latin America. Even when there are laws in place enabling intervention in those homes where violence is present, many look the other way. Others are so afraid of the justice and penal system they figure it's better to leave things the way they are. Slowly, shelters for women and children have begun to appear in some places, never near enough to take in all that need them, but even these slow changes have not been due to the church's initiative for the most part. I still hear in my therapist's office how women have been told by their pastors to return to a violent husband and be a submissive wife because divorce is not an option. "If you will just be a better wife, give him more sex, cook better, care for the children better, be more submitted, and continue to pray more, he will change." The insinuation is that the husband can do what he likes, and the wife must put up with it in the name of submission.

This is an area where churches must begin to change their ways. Violence is not an acceptable lifestyle, married or not. The Lord has called us to live in peace, not in violence. The *machismo* in our Latin churches cannot continue to have its way in our churches. Reconciliation is not an option as long as the chance of high-risk behavior is still present. Pastors should have the fear of the Lord in their hearts before they insist that a wife return to a violent husband. Too often, these women have died at the hands of their spouses.

Another situation that often brings people to the reconciliation room is "because of the children". There have been a lot of long-term studies on the effects of divorce on children, with conflicting results, but one thing is clear: living in an atmosphere of violence, constant conflict, disruption and instability is not healthy for children. Since children are ferociously obedient, they will learn to behave like their parents. When we stay together for the children's sake, we are telling them in subtle ways that this is an acceptable way to live. Marriage is a covenant between two adult people, and if we really want to be good to our children, we need to be good to our spouse.

Maintaining a marriage in name only, or keeping up the appearances for the sake of the children is questionable. Usually, the real reason lies somewhere else, with certain unmentioned fears, such as aging alone, not finding someone else out there with whom I could fit better, not being able to make it financially, sexual issues... the list of excuses goes on. Children were never a good reason to get married. They are not a good reason for reconciliation.

People who want to reconcile have to consider the cost of forgiveness. For some, they are not willing to really consider forgiving from their heart and this will kill any chances of a fruitful restoration of the marriage. Some marriages have ended or are on hold for very serious reasons, such as violence or adultery or consistent verbal and emotional abuse. (Some patients complain more about the words than the beating...) True repentance and forgiveness is necessary for the marriage to be made new. Trust has been lost and will need to be developed over time, which is a really tough issue.

So, when is reconciliation an option? When both members of the marriage covenant are willing to pay the price of change. More of what didn't work before isn't going to repair the relationship. In the same way that it took both of them to marry, it takes them both to reconcile appropriately. It is so much easier to give up than work things out, but a healthy marriage is more than worth the price to pay.

Most couples cannot do this alone. Mediation, psychotherapy, counseling, the spiritual disciplines (prayer, fasting, Scripture, renewing the mind, etc.) are all important elements to consider when the couple requests help for reconciliation.

Forgiveness is an important step in this process. I often ask my patients to make a list of all of the things they need to forgive each other, and then they need to start forgiving them, event by event. This is a list they are not to show each other, but they need to make the decision to not hold these issues against each other any more. Sometimes I tell them to burn the list as a pleasing burnt offering to God, as a gesture of true forgiveness. In the same way that they can no longer find the bits of paper, they should no longer be able to find the events that triggered resentment and bitterness in the past.

Then I ask the couple to make a list of all of the things for which they need to ask forgiveness from the other. This is a list they will bring to my office, and they will go over it, item by item and ask their spouse for forgiveness. Repentance is a big part of reconciliation and this is often the deal breaker. When the spouse can see that the other is truly remorseful over what s/he has done, reconciliation begins to open its door. (See **Forgiveness and Reconciliation: Keeping it Simple,** in Marriage & Family: A Christian Journal, Vol.2 (2) pp. 171-174, 1999, for a complete description.)

The grace of God is bigger than all of our sins, and reconciliation is possible, but it requires a lot of hard work on the part of each one involved. It means having to learn new ways of relating to each, falling in love again, caring for each other in the ways they need to in order to feel loved. It means learning to honor each other and putting the needs of the other before one's own desires, something that really only works when both are committed to this. After all, the same things that go into a healthy reconciliation go into making a marriage work. The hard part of reconciliation is that the couple is starting in the negative column and will have to dig themselves out of that hole in order to move forward towards a truly healthy relationship. But those who have done all agree: it is really worth it.

A Christian Woman and Divorced

"So, now, Esly, would you tell us a little bit about what it is like to be a Christian woman and divorced?"

The words of the pastor rang out over an enormous silence. It seemed like everyone was holding their breath in church while I stepped up front. Slowly, I began to share a testimony that gave birth to a new ministry in my life: to the unmarried.

I spoke about how there are three basic feelings that we as unmarried women often feel: guilt, failure and inadequacy. (Men tend to sit in the unmarried pew of life for much shorter periods of time, but I'm sure they feel some o this themselves.)

Guilt is a really big deal. There seems to be something in the make-up of most women, married or not, that makes us latch on to any free-floating guilt flying around. We seem to have a specialized antenna for it. We pick it up, even if it doesn't belong to us!

We often blame ourselves for everything that went wrong in the marriage. "Maybe if I had tried harder…. Maybe if I had done this or that…." Our What-If Syndrome clicks into high gear and spirals down its negative route.

But the truth is that in any marriage, there is a covenant between two people, and when one of the two gives up on the relationship, for whatever reason, it is over. The couple may even continue living together for a while longer, but it's done. Unless the person decides to get back into the game, the marriage is dead. There isn't a whole lot more a person can do about it, but bury it. God may even resurrect it, but even that belies the fact that it had died at some point.

For some mysterious reason, especially in Latin culture, the blame for the failure of the marriage seems to find its way to women. Brothers and sisters in Christ insinuate that she didn't put up with enough, if she'd just tried harder, tried this, or tried that… even when husbands are unfaithful; it's *still* the woman's fault! "Ah, you weren't good to him in bed and that's why he went looking for someone else". Some of these words are offered with the best of intentions, but they still burn like brazen coals on the head of the forlorn and abandoned woman.

It is true that God hates divorce, but He doesn't hate the divorced. God tolerates divorce because of the hardness of our hearts. So we really need to show some compassion and mercy to those who are going through this difficult experience in their lives. Most people feel quite a large measure of guilt when a marriage ends. We don't need to heap it on...

Secondly, there is a great sense of failure....failing at one of life's greatest projects, something that will have lifelong consequences - for me, as well as for my children. Sometimes, even without meaning to, the unmarried person gets side-lined very easily. She doesn't fit with her married friends anymore ("God forbid she try to take *my* husband away!" is an unfortunate attitude that appears more often than most would admit). And usually, there weren't a lot of single friends on the scene at that point either.

At church, it is often easy to begin to feel like a second-class citizen, and some churches even go so far as to make sure that divorced people understand that they are no longer eligible for certain positions or groups, especially in Latin America. Few churches offer support groups for those who are struggling with divorce, and many singles groups are a label for matchmaking attempts. It is a sad fact that many churches are really not equipped to handle the divorced. (That said, we would like to take a moment to applaud all those churches that have really made an effort to reach out to the divorced.)

Thirdly, many divorced people carry a feeling of inadequacy. How does one develop the new role of divorced? It is a totally new role to be learned, and at times it is intimidating, daunting and overwhelming. A divorce brings so many changes with it! There is much to be learned and few people who can really walk us through it.

A Virtuous Woman: Who can Find?

As a Brazilian woman and a Christian who went through a divorce, I had ample time to think through many of the issues I was forced to deal with. Reading through Proverbs 31, I began to wonder if divorced women would ever be considered virtuous. All I had ever heard on this topic were sermons praising virtuous – married – women. It is such an overly developed role in Latin America that oftentimes the "mother of my children" completely dominates all of the other roles of women.

On the other hand, no one describes a divorced woman as being virtuous. To the contrary, there tends to be a certain air of suspicion hovering over her, as if she were some kind of debtor or perhaps suffers from some fatal moral wrong, even when the initiative of the divorce was not hers.

Does a divorce take away a woman's virtue? Is a woman considered virtuous because of her civil status? Because she is married? Is her virtue conferred on her, because she has a man in her life and is therefore a "derived" virtue? Certainly not! But oftentimes, divorced women are often treated that way. Although all divorces are the result of sin (if the two parties involved could live perfectly together there would be no divorces!) it does not mean that everyone involved has lost their virtue.

One of the most common issues we deal with in Latin America with regard to women and virtue has to do with their state of motherhood and its meaning for marriage. It seems that everyone has permission to be a mother, although everyone prefers she does this within the confines of marriage. Even so, the number of single mothers is astounding and growing, and the stigma is shrinking.

Due to certain religious influences, motherhood is pretty close to sainthood. A mother is expected to put up with just about everything as long as it ensures the "good of the children" – bad marriages and domestic violence included. Mothers are lauded and praised for all of their sacrifices in raising the children because this is a sign of a virtuous woman who gives her life for her children. Women who "stick it out" with their philandering husbands are especially admired. Even husbands sheepishly appreciate all that their wives have had to put up with from them.

With the advent of the feminist movement, many women - even in Latin America - have moved into the work force and taken up men's traditional roles However, we see none of the opposite happening amongst the men: they are not longing to come home and wash dishes or care for sick children, or cook a meal every night or vacuum the floors. Women have now been saddled with a double work load: inside and outside the home. In some groups, the message is, "it's OK for you to work outside the home as long as your housework gets done as well and the children are cared for". It seems that working an outside job were a special concession.

So... within this context, a divorce takes away the virtue of a woman who should have put up with everything... she goes from being a virtuous sacrificial woman and turns into a "quitter" who deserts her post.

Yet this is not the example of Jesus. In him, we see a *man* (not a woman!) who give ups his life for his Bride, the Church, and who willingly takes on the sacrifice of his family. We see a tender Jesus, when tenderness is often equated with women. We see a Jesus who cries, when men are taught that "big boys don't cry". We see Jesus holding children in his lap, and blessing them, and not delegating child-rearing to women because "they are more sensitive and better understand how to care for children" (as one distinguished gentleman once told me...) We see Jesus speaking with women as equals and dignifying them in an ancient world where women were a notch higher than slaves. But we see a man, *a man*, who sacrifices all – even his life – for his family.

What Jesus teaches us about men is the opposite of what we see in our *machista* society, where woman are expected to put up, shut up and give up everything for the sake of the husband and children, or risk losing their "virtuous" status.

In fact, women who are divorced become prey for other men. The common myth is that since women have "tasted sex" in marriage, they can no longer do without it, so there is no lack of offers to "help them out with their hormones". Even Christian men are known to make these offers as well. It seems that in our Latin society, marriage still "protects" women and keeps them "virtuous" (faithful) and far away from the preying eyes of other men. It seems that divorce exposes them to this new and hidden danger.

So besides laying the heavy burden of insinuating that a woman failed by not being able to hang on to her husband, society and the church often condemn her for not having held her marriage together no matter what the cost. And the result is a loss of "virtue"…

But who is to say that divorced women aren't virtuous? Returning to the words of Proverbs 31… Divorced women are still good mothers – "her lamp does not go out at night"; good business people – "she sees a piece of land and buys it; she works hard – "doesn't eat of the bread of idleness"; and is a good manager – she gives orders to her servants. Obviously, divorced women do all of these things.

But the one thing a virtuous woman is NOT supposed to do is give her life for her children… *that* is the example of Jesus.

The Church and the Divorced

I don't believe that anyone would argue that God's perfect design for marriage does include divorces. We know that God hates divorce even though He doesn't hate divorced people! God does not quit loving people just because they divorce, although in many churches, this has unconsciously become part of the insinuated message. It would be totally incongruent with God's character for him to stop loving people who sinned. The whole point of the Gospel – the Good News! – is that God is *for* sinners, and not against them. And this includes divorced sinners as well.

God never intended for people to divorce, but then, He never intended for people to sin. Divorce is just one more of the consequences of the Fall. Jesus told the Pharisees that divorce had only been permitted in the law given to Moses because of the hardness of men's hearts. (And who can argue that people's hearts are still hard?) Yet, surprisingly, the writ of divorce that was to be given a woman when her husband divorced her was intended to protect her, and not harm her. Men who repudiated their wives were ordered to give her a bill of divorce so that she could legally remarry and re-organize her life without being in an adulterous relationship. In Jewish thought, to this day, a divorce always points to the possibility of a new marriage. In fact, the *ketubah*, or marriage license, stipulated how the woman would be protected, what were her rights and her inheritance in case of divorce. IF a man decided to divorce her, she had legal standing and protection to claim what had been arranged in her *ketubah*.

However, over time and over many cultural changes, with the advent of Greek influence that slowly took over the original Hebraic Church, repudiation and divorce began to change from their Jewish comprehension to the Greek one: from the possibility of breaking the marriage bond through divorce and the subsequent permission for remarriage to the traditions developed, especially in the Roman Catholic Church that marriage is a sacrament and the marriage bond can *never* be broken. (Almost all of the Church was Jewish for the first ten years of its existence. Gentile believers were the absolute exception until Peter had the vision that led him to meet Cornelius, and Paul was called to preach to the Gentiles.)

As I struggled with aspects of these issues myself, the bottom-line question became: is divorce the unpardonable sin? Can the Church have ex-assassins that were saved and redeemed in her midst? Can she have ex-alcoholics? ex-gays? ex-adulterers? And in most cases, people will say yes! God's grace reaches out to all of these. But it seemed that there was no room for the ex-married. In many churches, divorce meant the end of ministerial careers, the extinguishment of any hope for a future marital relationship, and the condemnation into some kind of relationship limbo that limited and restricted people who had had no say in whether or not they *wanted* to be divorced.

So do divorced people lose their salvation? Are they beyond the reach of God's grace? Are they now unworthy of their calling into the Kingdom of God? Have they in some way become second-class citizens?

Although divorce must break the heart of God, as all of our sins do, the doctrine of forgiveness and grace that is found in our Bibles teach us that forgiven sin is forgotten sin. Although we must live with the consequences of our sin, theologically, in the eyes of God, if we have confessed our sins, brought our hearts into godly repentance, and made amends as best we can, we are forgiven of God. Our slate is wiped clean, and our sins are thrown into the Sea of Forgetfulness. Paul states that there is now no condemnation for those who are in Christ Jesus (Rm. 8:1).

If this is true for so many other sins that church members would never argue about, why is it so hard to apply this to the sin of divorce? God does not have first- and second-class citizens. He calls us friends, not slaves. He calls us children, not servants. (Personally, I would not mind being God's slave as long as I got to be around him, yet He does not give us this option... amazing!!) We only enter the Kingdom of God as a child, and no one asks us what our marriage status is at the Pearly Gates, but rather, what is your relationship with Jesus?

Perhaps it is prudent to go back to some of the basics: what is the Church's function in the world? We are called to be light to the world, to show The Way (Jesus). We are to mirror God's love to the world through our lives and our relationships (which is why mirroring broken relationships through divorce hurts the Church). However, we are called to be a healing community, to reach out to the hurting and offer the balm of Gilead to the broken-hearted. We are not called to be legalists. God will judge our hearts, our behavior and our attitudes. Jesus affirmed that we would be judged in the same way we judged others. Personally, I stand in need of a tremendous amount of mercy and grace, which is why I work hard at offering that to others as well. Human judgment heals very little, whereas love covers a multitude of sins.

Over the years, as I recovered from my divorce in the midst of maintaining my relationship with the church, I picked up on many issues that were hurtful to strugglers like me. First of all, there really was an unconscious prejudice against the single and the single again. For the never-married the message was, "You were just not good enough to land a catch." To the divorced it was: "You were just not good enough to hang on to your spouse." In both cases, people walk away feeling worthless, on top of their own self-condemnation.

Undeniably, our churches have a growing number of divorced people. Whereas when I grew up, the divorced were the exception, now they are often the rule in many churches. Although some churches have tried to reach out to the single-agains, more often than not these meetings turn into crude match-making situations or groups of "unclaimed promises" wall-flowered for life. It is often hard for the divorced to fit into the groups that the churches offer: they are no longer a couple, yet they have children (sometimes). At times when the children visit the other spouse they are more like singles. When the children are home, they are more like the married (with all of the obligations and few of the pleasures of married life, as my dad would say).

Sometimes well-intentioned church members say things like, "I am praying for you, and that God would restore your life. It must be terrible to be in a broken home." Others insist on praying for reconciliation even in the face of the fact that it could be life-threatening. Still others think that the only cure will be a new spouse. What comes across is that somehow we are incomplete persons if we are not married...

I am deeply convinced that for the most part, these kinds of comments are borne out of the people's lack of information, or their insensitivity to the divorced's plight rather than evil intent. As we educate the Church about the consequences of divorce and how church members can be instruments of healing in this process, the response for the most part tends to be positive.

So, how can the Church be sensitive and caring to the plight of those who are going through or have gone through a divorce?

Perhaps the first step is to open a space where divorced people can be safe, not just physically safe, but emotionally safe to share their pain, their suffering, their hurt. There is so much confusion and a sense of lostness in those who are going through a marriage break-up. If the Church could just open her arms, take these hurting people in, and help them recover, so many could be won for the Lord. A ministry of consolation would go a long way in binding up the broken-hearted. Coming alongside those who are in pain, and confusion, with prayer or practical help would enable us to fill our churches with new believers. People who hurt are often at their most vulnerable moment, and most open to receiving the word of comfort that can only be found in the Lord Jesus. It is true that the church would be filled with these redeemed sinners, but then, what other kind of church is there?

On the other hand, people who are going through these crises are a lot of work. They tend to be unstable. Not only do their emotions go up and down, but so do their circumstances!!! Some literally have daily challenges for a role they are only now just learning to develop. Being a sounding-board for them, just listening can be hugely helpful.

God puts the solitary in families (Ps 68:6) Being around other families is healing and helpful. Perhaps there are churches that could "adopt" the divorced in some ways. The Church has so much to offer: friendship, and understanding, and care. Adoption can go along way in the process of recovery for divorced people. It is often hard to go on a family vacation with a 3 year-old. This is where church members can practice the gift of hospitality: invite the divorced into their homes, share Sunday meals with them, and help them with minor tasks and strategies (getting a car fixed can be a huge challenge for some women!), invite them to do things together as a family. The church family is not called a *family* for nothing!!

I want to publicly thank the church that took me in when I was going through my divorce. Friends would invite me to meals with a table full of friends. I loved hearing the children yack (with my daughter), the father of the house pray, shooting the breeze with brothers and sisters. It was so nice to be a part of a family, even if it lasted only for a few hours. These families cared for me, consoled and comforted me over a period of months and years (recovery takes a long time!) I haven't forgotten friends who helped me care for my daughter, and served as role models for her, especially when her father was absent. I'm always sorry to hear that others weren't as blessed as I was…

Let's also let the Lord take the initiative (or not) as to re-marriage. Some people will marry again, and others will not. Let's be sensitive as we deal with this issue, and take into consideration some of the historical changes that doctrine has gone through in its development before we jump to conclusions.

Finally, we need to remember that there is life after divorce. I thought my life had come to an end when my marriage failed (I wasn't even thirty!), but God had other plans for me. He showed me that I was still worthwhile, even as a *divorced* human being. And over the years, He has restored everything the locusts have eaten (Joel 2:25), many times over.

Shall We Marry Again?

As Christians, is this an option?

For many, it is not, as we have seen historically. But the truth is that more and more Christians are divorcing and the great majority of them are marrying again. Unfortunately, the divorce/remarriage rate among Christians is not that different from that of non-Christians.

Although divorces are sometimes like therapeutic abortions – done to save the life of one of the people involved – or miscarriages – the divorced spouse had no say in the matter - they interrupt the normal flow of family life. They are not part of God's perfect intention for humankind, but since this had become a daily fact in the family life of our church members we need to look at the issue of remarriage as well.

Once the theological sticking points are settled, and this is usually a person as well as a pastoral issue, then we need to look at the emotional issues that go into a new marriage. Here are some pointers to think about for those who are considering remarriage.

First of all, finish "divorcing".

1. Remember to grieve well. It is important to take no unfinished business into a second marriage. Studies show that 75% of second marriages fail. Do your best to finish the grief work so that it doesn't get in the way of a possible second relationship.

2. Spend a season of repentance, Biblical meditation and confession to God over what has happened. "Examine all things. Hang on to that which is good."

3. Don't "tread water" waiting for "Prince Charming" to come along. Many people think that after a marriage ends one is supposed to do something just to get by until the new marriage arrives, when "real life" will begin again. Nothing could be further from the truth! The truth is that the prince may never come and then what? We cannot afford to put all of our emotional "eggs" into one basket.

4. Acknowledge the fear of a new commitment. Lots of people are afraid of making a mistake the second time, and no one wants the heartbreak of a divorce *again*.

5. Work on yourself. Seek counseling or psychotherapy. Figure out how you can become a better person. Heal the hurt places in your life: both those caused by the divorce as well as those you've been carrying around from childhood (and may well have contributed towards the end of the marriage.)

6. Build a good single life for yourself. Have an interesting life! Do things you've wanted to and couldn't, learn new skills, enjoy your own company, grow in the Lord. Learn to appreciate aloneness as opposed to loneliness. At one point I made a decision that I wanted to have such a rich life that a man would have to be very special to enrich it more. (Ken did!)

Then... you can consider remarriage.

1. **Is this really an option for you?** Some people desire to remarry, others do not, and some are laissez-faire about it.

Some people do not desire to remarry because of their age, or because they have small children and they do not want to expose them to step-parents. Others are too afraid (and need to cast out their fear with God's perfect love, whether or not they ever decided to marry again). Fear is not a good (nor godly) lifestyle.

Others can think about nothing else but remarriage. That is not a good motivation either. Our life is not "incomplete" without a mate.

Perhaps the best choice is to leave it in the Lord's hands. When we can get to the point where - "whether I marry or not is God's decision" -we are reaching a point of real maturity and recovery from our divorce.

2. All of the good things we learned about **choosing a mate** the first time are still valid for the second round. Perhaps the second time is even a bit more difficult because with children involved, one needs to be "pickier". Our future spouse will need to be a person committed to the Lord and committed to this relationship. Many people think that because their first spouse was a Christian and their marriage failed that it doesn't matter the second time whether s/he is or not... this is not good thinking. It is still important to not be unequally yoked.

Perhaps the first marriage was an unequal yoke and that was one of the reasons for the break-up? Then let's learn the lesson this time around…

3. **Listen to your children**. It is important to spend time together with everyone. Although we don't recommend taking children along on first dates, once a relationship gets serious, they need to be included slowly if marriage is in sight. Surprising children with a marriage is one of the sure-fire ways of gaining their resentment and assuring a bad start to the second marriage.

Children have good antennae. If they don't like The Candidate, pay attention. Find out why. Sometimes they see/perceive things that are important and that you need to take into consideration. Maybe it's a sign that you should slow down.

But children don't ultimately make those decisions. Marriage is an adult decision that needs to be made by adults, and children will need to be taught to respect that. However, be fair by not imposing decisions, but trying to reach consensus as much as possible. After all, with time they will leave home and you are the one who will stay in the marriage.

4. **Listen to God**. Many people say they will do this, but when they are in the throes of romantic love, most find it very difficult to listen to the Lord should He say… no. It is amazing the kind of bargaining, denial and other manipulative extremes people will go to in order to "convince" themselves, God or others that this is a good match. If you are not willing to end this relationship should God say so, then the relationship has become more important than God. You are on thin ice.

Remember that the Lord wants only what is good for us, and He sees the big picture. He cannot desire something for us that will ever harm us or do us evil. If we let Him choose, it will ultimately work out for good. We should always be ready to receive whatever comes from His hands.

God is a Matchmaker

"One year from now, you will be married."

I almost fell out of bed as these words came to me while I was in prayer. I didn't know what to think: was I hallucinating, or was my desire for remarriage so great that I was beginning to imagine things? Or perhaps it really was the gentle nudge of the Holy Spirit inside of me, encouraging my heart.

I opened my journal, wrote the phrase in and dated it. I figured that if it truly came from the Lord, then it would come to pass. And if it wasn't, I needed to learn how to be more sensitive to the voice of God. As I closed my journal, I reflected on so many of the things that had happened to me in the pilgrimage of the last few years.

Soon after I signed my divorce papers, my daughter and I moved into our own apartment. As I stood in the empty living room I was totally overwhelmed with the challenge of raising a three-year-old by myself. In one of my moments of deepest anguish, I cried to the Lord and said, "You are a God of peace, and harmony and reconciliation. Why have you allowed this to happen? Why will I have to raise my child alone?" And as I cried, the Lord spoke quietly to my heart: *"I have a husband prepared for you, but it's not for now. It's for a long time off. Meanwhile, I want you to make the best life possible for you and your daughter and I will be with you."* So with this promise, I dried my eyes, and started fixing up the apartment.

Life was not easy. Every month I had to pay the rent. I had uneven income as a psychotherapist and some months seemed to have more month than money! One night, the Lord led me to Isaiah 54, where it says that our Maker will be our husband. Fine by me... so I prayed, "Lord, if you are my Husband then you are now in charge of the rent." And every month it got paid. New patients would arrive, just enough to make the bills, but everything got paid.

Once I slipped up and asked my ex-husband to help with a few unexpected health bills for Raquel. I was livid when I hung up the phone because of the way he talked to me. I turned to the Lord, and said, "Did you hear what he said to me?! What a terrible way to talk to me!" And that very moment, the Lord answered, *"Why did you ask him for money? Aren't I your Husband? Have you or Raquel ever lacked for anything since I took on this responsibility? When you need money, you come and talk to Me."*

I was so embarrassed and ashamed. I confessed my mistake to the Lord and learned my lesson. Our God is a *jealous* God: He does not share His responsibilities with anyone else.

Some years later, when I received an invitation to move to Ecuador, Raquel and I were ready to take on the challenge: a new country, a new language, a new school for Raquel and a new job for me. I felt a little like Abraham who left his country and countrymen to go to a foreign land. But we were excited about this new opportunity.

My curiosity was especially piqued when one of my patients in Brazil said to me in one of our good-bye sessions: "This time in therapy has been very important to me. Not only have you helped me with my marriage and my children, but you have also been a sister in Christ. My only consolation as you leave is knowing that God has a husband prepared for you there." I got very quiet, surprised at his words, pondering them in my heart like Mary.

A few months after this experience, I was in Quito, exhausted with the effort of trying to take in all of the changes. I was a single mom, trying to care for this young child and my responsibilities weighed on me. One night, as I prayed, I remembered the promise the Lord had made to me some six years earlier. "Lord, I know that you can send me a husband when I am 65 years old and you will have been faithful to your word. But I would like to ask that if it is possible, that you send him soon, while my daughter can benefit from the experience. She will soon enter adolescence and needs a good man who will love her and care for her as she grows up. I am sure that the man you send me as a husband will also be good to her." That was the moment I heard His still small voice say, *"A year from today you will be married."*

Several weeks went by and as the loneliness grew, I signed up for some dinners offered by a local English-speaking church.

(Spanish was still a challenge!) I thought it would be a good way to make new friends, but walking into a room full of strangers has always been one of those things that absolutely terrifies me. So I said to myself in the mirror, "Self, you can't make new friends sitting here at home. Make an effort. Go on. No one is going to bite you and perhaps you will even meet some interesting people. Who knows, you might even *enjoy* the experience!" So I went out and bought a quart of ice cream and climbed the long stairwell to the pastor's apartment. Dinner had begun and I sat alongside others who had come with the purpose of making new friends as well.

I sat between the pastor and a middle-aged gentleman of nice appearance. We were asked to introduce ourselves and share a bit about our lives. It wasn't long before we were all at ease, and it was my turn to share.

I found out that the gentleman next to me was called Ken, and he had very interesting stories to share about China, where he grew up, a child of missionary parents in the old China Inland Mission. They were forced to leave some time after the Communist Revolution and Ken finally arrived in England with his parents at age eight, after a long, slow and dangerous trek to Hong Kong from southwest China.

As he spoke, I thought to myself, his wife must be traveling and he took advantage of a good meal to make new friends. He was Canadian and had lived in the country for over 25 years. But halfway through dinner, he commented that his wife had passed away a few months before and there was a respectful silence as we took in this piece of information. It turned out that this was his first attempt at coming back into in the social stream after Joy had died. It seemed his joy had died, too. He looked raw. I could tell he was hurting because he still bled all over.

As all of us said our good-byes, we took note of new phone numbers and promised to stay in touch. Ken said he would call me some time, and I thought that could be a lot of fun. But I could tell I was reticent as well. When I got home, I had a little heart-to-heart talk with the Lord. "Did You see what an interesting man that Ken is?" And I felt the Lord smile…

But Ken didn't call and I had several international trips that were part of my work responsibilities. Sometimes we would run into each other at the evening service at church and chat for a few moments. Ken seemed to be a really special guy, and at my age, there were not a lot of "available" single men, widowed or otherwise. But I had already said to the Lord that if Ken was the man He had prepared for me, that was fine, but I wasn't going to lift a finger to make it happen. He had to come to my front door under his own steam. I had come to firmly believe in what Pr. Derek Prince said: that God was a matchmaker[1]. He explained in his book by that title that God takes the initiative to make people meet. When He sees that it is not good for someone to be alone, He brings two people together. God didn't need my help for that. It had to be God's initiative. However, my heart would skip a beat every time I saw Ken...

The Bible begins (Gen. 2:22) and ends (Revelation) with the story of marriages. In fact, as Derek Prince well points out in his book, it is God himself who takes the initiative that people should wed. He creates Eve even before Adam asks for her. The two come together as a direct desire of the heart of God. We see this pattern repeat itself many times over. Rebecca is presented to Isaac. Ruth comes to Boaz. Jacob meets Rachel in one of the most beautiful love affairs in the Bible. And finally, Jesus is awaiting his bride, the Church, whom God took the initiative to form.

One Sunday night, several months after that first dinner where we met, Ken came and talked to me at the church door. I could tell he wanted to say something and didn't know where to start. A bit like an adolescent on a first date, he turned and asked me, "Would you like to go out and have a cup of coffee?" And I replied, "Right now?" He smiled. "Yes, why not?" So I called up a friend who was watching Raquel and asked her to keep her a bit longer. "I'll tell you later, but it's for a good cause!!" We laughed, months later, as we recalled the events that finally led up to our marriage.

The pizza we shared that night brought new opportunities to see each other. Sometimes the four of us would go out: Raquel,

---

[1] Prince, Derek y Prince, Ruth (1986) God is a Matchmaker. Grand Rapids: Chosen Books

who was nine by then, and Scott, Ken's teenage son. These were good moments for us to see how all of us got along. We were good friends until the night he planted a good-night kiss on my lips and then ran off like a frightened jackrabbit!! After that, we slowly began talking about a future together.

There were many obstacles. The organization that Ken worked with did not take kindly to the idea of their members marrying divorcées. It was not in their policy. One night, Ken came to visit and he said, "...either they change their minds – and I think it's easier for the laws of the Medes and Persians to change! – or God will provide a new job for me where your divorce is not an issue, or this relationship does not come from God and should end." I really admired his attitude, so we prayed and committed it to the Lord.

A few weeks later, we went out with a pastor and his wife. They shared their story with us and it was so similar that we were totally taken aback. His first wife had also died of cancer, like Joy, when the pastor was about Ken's present age. He had married a divorcée. After dinner, we went to Ken's house for coffee and dessert, and the pastor said to Ken, "I have a word from the Lord for you. If a new opportunity appears for you to change positions, you are to take it. The Lord is going to change the direction of your life." This was highly unusual behavior for a pastor of his conservative denomination, se we were very perplexed, but knowing his care and love for us, we accepted.

The very next morning, an old friend of Ken's knocked on his door, and invited him to play racquetball. At the end of the game, Ken had a new job offer.

Months later, we went to Brazil to get married. We invited our friends and amongst them was the patient who had told me God had a husband waiting for me in Quito. It was the happiest day of my life. The church was full of friends who had seen me through the toughest parts of my life, and who had now come to rejoice in our happiness.

Some months later, we were facing some of the normal adjustments of marriage and a blended family. "Do we have to drag this man along with us everywhere we go?" Raquel asked me one night. Although I had my concerns, Ken slowly won her over with his love and care for her, and became a wonderful influence in her life.

A few months later, as I was going through my prayer journal, counting my blessings as I sometimes do, I found the entry with the promise the Lord had made to me a year before in Quito. As I did the numbers, I realized that lacking *eight days to the year*, I had said my wedding vows.

God, our holy matchmaker, had been faithful to his promise.

Divorce, the Law and Jesus, By Walter L. Callison
Revised August 20, 2012

Are people who are divorced and married to another living in adultery?

How did we ever begin to read "whosoever divorces his wife" into those places where Jesus literally said "whosoever puts away or abandons, his wife"?

It is easy to preach against divorce, but difficult for a church to be constructive in providing preparation for marriage.

Divorce and remarriage are topics of much debate. The purpose of the following article is to invite the reader to reassess the church's attitude toward remarriage. We welcome your comments and opinions on the content of this article.

"*For the law was given by Moses, but grace and truth came by Jesus Christ.*" (John 1:17). Grace. Did grace come by Jesus Christ to those suffering marital tragedy, even as much grace as was provided by Old Testament law? Surely, we affirm, *grace and truth* did come by Jesus Christ. Then how does grace abound to those who have suffered the tragedy of a marriage failure and divorce?

Christ did more than teach with words. He also taught with his life. Christ brought new ideas to his followers, rejecting their ancient "*eye for an eye*" and "*tooth for a tooth*" doctrines, encouraging love for those not their own, lifting up women from the status of "*things*" to recognition as people. Yet he also taught respect for the old Jewish law.

When we study what he said about divorce, we must also study the life he lived among those of broken marriages, as well as what he taught about Jewish law, especially their divorce law.

But what about his words? If a divorced person is remarried, what about the words, "*Whosoever putteth away his, wife and marrieth another committeth adultery*" (Luke 16:18)? We could emulate the compassionate and forgiving nature of Christ, as he sent the woman at the well into Samaria to be his witness. But do his words deny his actions? Are people who are divorced and married to another living in adultery? Are they forbidden service to Christ?

We also must hear the words of the Apostle Paul. *"A bishop then must be blameless, the husband of one wife"* (I Tim. 3:2). Does he speak of a person who has been divorced and remarried?

Luke records only one comment, and a very concise one, on this subject:

"And it is easier for heaven and earth to pass, than one tittle of the law to fail. Whosoever putteth away his wife, and marrieth another, committeth adultery; and whosoever marrieth her that is put away from her husband committeth adultery" (Luke 16:17-18).

Concise. But Jesus did make it clear that the Old Testament had something significant to say. There is a law! When asked by the Pharisees, in the Gospel of Mark, *"Is it lawful for a man to. put away his wife?"* (Mark 10:2), Jesus answered, *"What did Moses command you?" (Mark 10:3). "They said, Moses suffered to write a bill of divorcement"* (Mark 10:4). There is a law.

The law is found in Deuteronomy 24:1-4, and at the time Christ lived, Flavius Josephus, who also lived then, paraphrased it and referred to it as the*"law of the Jews"*:

"He that desires to be divorced from his wife for any cause whatsoever, (and many such causes happen among men), let him in writing give assurance that he will never use her as his wife any more; for by this means she may be at liberty to marry another husband, although before this bill of divorce be given, she is not to be permitted so to do..." **Antiquities of the Jews (The Life and Work of Flavius Josephus)**, Book IV, Ch. VIII, Sec. 23, p. 134; (tr. Wm. Whiston; Holt, Rinehart, and Winston, NY).

Here is the law from Deuteronomy:

"When a man hath taken a wife, and married her, and it come to pass that she find no favour in his eyes, because he hath found some uncleanness in her: then let him write her a bill of divorcement, and give it in her hand, and send her out of his house. And when she is departed out of his house, she may go and be another man's wife" (Deut. 24:1.2).

The law was still around in the time of Christ. We must, therefore, deal with the *"tittles"* of the law. The Bible only records ONE divorce. **God said he did it.** In Jeremiah 3, God reminded Judah that she was heading for trouble. Israel had already been taken captive. God told Jeremiah to warn Judah that she had witnessed her sister Israel's infidelity and had seen God give her a bill of divorce and send her away; and yet she did not fear (Jer. 3:6-8).

There were other things men did with their wives. Many men of old married more than one wife, and without bothering about divorce. Some of these were God's servants; Solomon, David, Abraham, and Esau, for example. Heroes of God's revelation, but also products of their culture.

If he did not divorce her, what did a man of those days do with a wife when he took another? He *put her away*. There is a word for that in the Old Testament, the Hebrew word *"shalach."* It is different than the Hebrew word for *"divorce,"* which is *"keriythuwth"* (Jer. 3:8 above) literally means excision, a cutting of the marital bonds; legal divorce was written, as commanded in Deuteronomy 24, and permitted subsequent marriage. *"Shalach"* is usually translated *"to put away."* Women were *"put away"* when their men married others, *put away* to be available if needed or wanted again, *put away* to become mere property, as slaves, or *put away* in total dismissal; it was a cruel day for women. They were *"put away"* in favor of another, but not given a divorce and the right to marry again. This word described a cruel tradition, common, but contrary to Jewish law.

Some of the hardships and terror experienced by women who were *"put away"* can be seen as, this Hebrew word *"shalach"* is described in the *Langenscheid Pucket Hebrew Dictionary* (McGraw-Hill, 1969) *"to let loose, roaming at large, to be scared, abandoned, forsaken."*

J. B. Phillips, in his book of meditations *For This Day* (Word, 1975) wrote:

"The Christian faith took root and flourished in an atmosphere almost entirely pagan, where cruelty and sexual immorality were taken for granted, where slavery and the inferiority of women were almost universal, while superstition and rival religions with all kinds of bogus claims existed on every hand."

God hated this *"putting away."* Malachi, the prophet, broken-heartedly pleaded with God's people to stop the practice. Hear Malachi plead with them. The word translated *"putting away"* in Mal. 2:16 is not the Hebrew word for *"divorce"* but it is *"shalach,"* put away. Hear Malachi respond to leaders who asked how they had dealt treacherously, and committed abomination in Israel, and profaned the holiness of the Lord.

*"Yet ye say, Wherefore? Because the Lord hath been witness between thee and the wife of thy youth against whom thou hast dealt treacherously: yet is she thy companion, and the wife of the covenant. And did not he make one? Yet had he the residue of the spirit. And wherefore one? That he might seek a godly seed. Therefore, take heed to your spirit, and let none deal treacherously against the wife of his youth. For the Lord, the God of Israel, saith that he hateth **putting away**"* (Mal. 2:14-16).

And Jesus came. And his words do not deny his actions! He spoke of this when he said, *"Whosoever putteth away his wife, and marrieth another, committeth adultery: and whosoever marrieth her that is put away from her husband committeth adultery"* (Luke 16:18). Whosoever does this commits adultery! This practice was cruel and was adulterous, but it was not divorce.

This New Testament word, translated *"put away"* in the King James Version, is a form of the Greek word *"apoluo."* It is the word in Greek, the language of the New Testament, which parallels the Hebrew word *"shalach" (put away).*

There is an Old Testament Hebrew word for divorce, *"keriythuwth,"* and a New Testament Greek word, "apostasion." The ***Arndt-Gingrich Lexicon of the New Testament*** cites usage of the word "apostasion" for the technical term for a bill or writing of divorce as far back as 258 B.C.

"Apoluo," the Greek word for putting away, was not technically divorce, though often used synonymously. In that time of total male domination, men often took additional wives, and did not provide a written release when they forsook wives and married others. The Jewish law demanding written divorce (Deut. 24:1.2) was largely ignored. If a man married another woman, so what? If a man *"put away" (apoluo)* his wife without bothering with a written divorce, who was going to object? The woman?

Jesus had some objections. Jesus even loved mistreated women! He told them that this earth would go up in smoke before the law requiring a written bill of divorce should fail (Lk. 16:17). And he said, when you put away a wife (without written divorce), and marry another (while still married), you are guilty of adultery

(Lk. 16:17). Moreover, she who is put away is in real trouble. She has no divorce paper. She is abandoned, but still married. She would commit adultery if she married again (Lk. 16:18).

The distinction between "*put away*" and "*divorce,*" between the Greek "*apoluo*" and "*apostasion*" is critical. "*Apoluo*" indicated that women were enslaved, put away, with no rights, no recourse; deprived of the basic right to monogamous marriage. "*Apostasion*" ended marriage and permitted a legal subsequent marriage. The paper makes a difference. "*Let him write her a bill of divorcement, and give it in her hand, and send her out of his house. And when she is departed out of his house, she may go and be another man's wife*" (Deut. 24:2). That was the law.

There are passages, other than Luke 16:17-18 (above) where Jesus spoke on this matter. They include Matt. 19:9, Mark 10:10-12 (where Mark records that Jesus laid down the same law for women as for men), and Matt. 5:32. Jesus used a form of the word "*apoluo*" eleven times in these passages. In every passage he forbade "*apoluo,*" **putting away**. He never forbade giving "*apostasion,*" written divorce, required by Jewish law.

Should the Greek word *apoluo* be translated *divorce*? Kenneth S. Wuest in T*he New Testament, an Expanded Translation* always translated it"*dismissed*" or "*put away,*" never "*divorced.*" The old, and very literal *American Standard Version* always translated it "*put away.*" The *King James Version* translated it "*put away*" ten out of the eleven times Jesus used it. That eleventh instance seems to be the source of the problem. In 1611, in**ONE** place the *King James* translators wrote "*divorced*" instead of "*put away.*" In Matt. 5:32, they wrote, "*and whosoever shall marry her that is***divorced** *committeth adultery.*" The word is not the Greek word "*apostasion*" (divorce), but is a form of that same Greek word "*apoluo,*" which did not include a writing of divorce for the woman. She, technically, would still be married.

Matt. 19:3-10 records the Pharisees taunting Jesus about this matter, asking him, "*Is it lawful for a man to put away his wife for every cause?*" He responded that marriage is a permanent relationship, and said, "*Whatsoever God hath joined together, let not man put assunder*" (Matt. 19:6).

They then asked, *"Why did Moses then command to give a writing of divorcement (apostasion), and to put her away?"* (Matt. 19:7); Jesus answered. *"because of the hardness of your hearts!"* (Matt, 19:8). The first basic human right God gave us was the right to be married. No other companionship is adequate. Hard-hearted men unilaterally put away women and married others, considering themselves divorced, but leaving the women without recourse and deprived of that first basic human right. Human rights were for men only in those days. Jesus changed that! He demanded obedience to the law; he demanded equal marriage rights for women. Grace does abound in Jesus Christ!

Jesus told those men that to put away a wife and to marry another was adultery. Adultery! The law (Deut. 22:22) called for the death penalty for adultery, for both the woman and the man! That was bitter medicine for the men who did as they pleased with women. Matt. 19:10 records their shock: *"If the case of a man be so with his wife, it is not good to marry."* They did not live in a culture wherein a man was expected to live with only one woman for life, much less, give her equal rights if marriage failed.

How did we ever begin to read *"whosoever divorces his wife"* into those places where Jesus literally said *"whosoever puts away, or abandons, his wife"*?

It may be that the one place where *apoluo* was mistranslated *"divorced"* in 1611 started the whole process. The **American Standard Version** corrected the error in 1901. It never became popular enough to make much difference. Wuest was careful to avoid such mistakes, as noted earlier. But almost every thing that has ever come off a printing press has been influenced by the **King James Version** of the Bible, even Greek English lexicons, and most modern translators seem to be influenced by that one occurrence in it and translate *"apoluo"* as *"divorce,"* even though the meaning of the word does not include a writing on divorce *(apostasion)*. Now, tradition has taught us to record *"divorced"* in our minds, though our eyes actually read *"put away"* in the **King James Version.**

Is written divorce, as commanded in Deuteronomy, the solution to the cruel practice of *"putting away"*? The twenty-fourth chapter of Deuteronomy is evidence that, even as God heard the groaning of his people in Egypt and provided deliverance from slavery, he also heard the groans of enslaved women and provided deliverance from abuse by means of that tragic necessity, divorce; tragic because it ends that which should never end, marriage; necessary to protect the victims of those who do not obey the rules of our creator, all-mighty God. Necessary, originally, because men"*put away*" women, trapping them in illegal and adulterous multiple marriages. Divorce is Tragedy.

Divorce is a privilege, provided as a corrective for an intolerable situation, It is a privilege which can be, and often is, abused. Divorce is not a pretty picture in most cases, Loneliness, rejection, a deep sense of failure, loss of self-esteem, critical relatives, child care problems, property settlements--these concerns, and more confront the divorced.

Divorce can be more traumatic than the death of a mate. Grief following the death of a spouse is hard to bear, as is the grief of divorce. But a dead spouse does not keep coming back. The divorced one often does, thus prolonging and often renewing grief. Divorce is still only what it was in Jesus' day, a partial solution to a serious and cruel situation; and maybe the only reasonable solution. It may be necessary, but it is always a tragedy!

We might be able to prevent some divorces by tightening our divorce laws or by religious prohibitions against divorce, but such actions would not prevent broken marriages. When couples stay together only because of fear of the notoriety required by divorce laws, or because of church prohibitions, or "*for the sake of the children,*" tragedy can result. Disastrous marital triangles, domestic cruelty, child abuse, murder, and suicide are some of the documented consequences of marriage which had failed, but was not terminated. What a fearful choice! A broken home is a tragedy, but I will never forget a young man who put a gun barrel in his mouth and ended his marriage, his alternative to divorce. His church had forbidden divorce.

Our high divorce rate is not the real problem. Marriage failure comes first, and then divorce. The divorce rate is only an indicator of our high bad marriage rate. To correct this, we must do more than preach against divorce! It will be more difficult. It is easy to preach against divorce, but difficult for a church to be constructive in providing preparation for marriage and strengthening of marriages. Our challenge lies here!

Can a divorced person be ordained as a deacon or a preacher? The Apostle Paul, an educated man, knew the Greek word for "*divorce*" *(apostasion)*and knew his culture. He also knew Christ would accept anyone, even him, the "*chiefest of sinners*" (I Tim. 1:15), Unquestionably some early converts had multiple wives, slave wives, and concubines. Each of these relationships, though given the nicer title, polygamy, was adultery, Paul rejected the heads of such households as leaders in the church, The command to give a writing of divorcement in Deuteronomy 24 limited a man to only one wife and thus prohibited polygamy, and the adultery inherent in it. Paul seemed to concur fully when he said, "*A bishop then must be blameless, the husband of one wife*" (I Tim. 3:2). He rejected polygamy, not divorce.

Despite serious abuse, the divorce law (Deuteronomy 24) still has validity, Divorce is a radical solution to insurmountable marital problems. It ends all hope that the marriage might be saved, and declares publicly that the marriage has failed. This moment of truth can be shattering. Sin, related to this failure, must be confessed if there is to be any forgiveness, any peace with God, "*If we confess our sin, he is faithful and just to forgive us our sin, and to cleanse us from all unrighteousness*" (I John 1:9). This includes forgiveness for marital failure.

As opposed to putting away, written divorce, commanded by the law, provided a degree of human dignity for women subjected to cruel abuse, adulterous polygamy, and the whims of hard-hearted men. Nothing so flimsy as an oral "*I divorce you*" would do. Divorce declared the legal end of a marriage, thereby precluding any charge of adultery or bigamy should either party ever marry again. Divorce severed all marital ties and all control by the former spouse, Divorce demanded strict monogamy. Divorce prevented unilateral dismissal and preserved the basic right to be married. Divorce does the same today. Abandonment, desertion, putting away, or whatever one calls that hard-hearted forsaking of a wife for another, without divorce, was and is forbidden by the Lord Jesus himself (Mt. 19:9, Mt. 5:32, Mk. l0:11-12, Lk. 16:18).

For centuries much of the Christian community has interpreted these teachings of Jesus to say:

1) Divorce is absolutely not permitted, or at best, is permitted only in the case of admitted or proven adultery.
2) A divorced person is not allowed to marry again.
3) A divorced person who does marry again lives in adultery.
4) A person who is divorced cannot be ordained as a deacon or a minister.

Every one of these beliefs could be wrong. The first three are contrary to Mosaic Law and are based on scripture in which Jesus did not even use the Greek word for *"divorce"* *(apostasion)*; the fourth is based on scripture in which Paul did not use it. The word Jesus used was *"apoluo,"* to put away. This was the problem with which he dealt, not divorce.

A divorced person must have great grace and determination to serve in a church which holds to the four positions listed above. How can this be, when the church is the body of Christ on earth, to function and to serve as he did, in person?

Christ, who once wept over Jerusalem, must look down from heaven and weep over us, He came, and called Simon the Zealot, a radical anti-Roman, and Matthew, a hated lackey of Rome, a pair as incompatible as any you could find in America today; but he put them to work, together, in his kingdom. Then he went to Samaria, revealed himself to a woman with a shameful background of marital failures, and sent her out to share the revelation of God in Christ, as if she were as good as anyone else. **He must weep when he sees us wasting our time trying to figure out who we can disbar from serving him in his church.**

Jesus openly ministered to all who came to him. Yet many of our divorced friends are afraid of our churches. They know what we say the Bible teaches about divorce. Can we be right and so unlike Christ? Do our traditional interpretations separate us from people whom Christ would have received? If so, we must be wrong. He came to save sinners. The only people he ever rejected were the self-righteously religious. Is our understanding of his words correct if it does not square with his life? Divorced people are real people! For centuries churches have excluded these people from fellowship and usefulness, from joy and equality, even from salvation; people for whom Christ died. Whether or not divorce is sin, this certainly is. May God grant us the grace to mediate that grace which did come in Jesus, Christ to the divorced.

Reprinted by permission, granted May 6, 2003 from the author.

Walter L. Callison was born on March 7, 1928 and passed away on July 7, 2009 in Yates Center, Kansas. He died less than two weeks after his wife of 62 years went to heaven.

About the Author

Esly Regina Carvalho, Ph.D. is a Brazilian-American clinical psychologist and author, as well as a presenter in great demand. Having been raised in the US, she also lived in Ecuador and Bolivia, besides her native Brazil, which has led her to be perfectly fluent in English, Portuguese and Spanish.

Esly has been committed to integrating different fields in a way that is helpful to both laypeople as well as professionals in a hands-on kind of way. In the field of Psychodrama, she has written a Manual in Spanish, published a compendium of professionals articles on Sociodrama and Sociometry, and more recently, integrated EMDR (Eye Movement Desensitization and Reprocessing) with Role Therapy, resulting in her book, *Healing the Folks Who Live Inside,* available in paperback and kindle, in all three languages. Her Bibliodrama Manual integrates techniques from Psychodrama with Bible stories.

Integrating Psychotherapy with principles of Biblical counseling led her to write several books in Spanish and Portuguese on topics such as divorce and remarriage (*Single Again, When the Bond Breaks, Cuando se rompe el vínculo,* available in Spanish and Portuguese), emotional healing (*Alas de sanidad*), leadership (*Cuidemos nuestros líderes,* in Spanish and Portuguese) and marriage (*Hacer el amor en todo lo que se hace*).

Also available are books integrating emotional growth and Biblical principles (*Caderno de Oração, Compañeros de yugo, Jogos Dramáticos para Cristãos*), available in Spanish and Portuguese.

Originally trained in Psychodrama and Group Psychotherapy in Brazil, Esly passed her exams with the American Board of Examiners in Psychodrama and Sociometry, with distinction, and is a *Fellow* of the American Society of Group Psychotherapy and Psychodrama (ASGPP).

Having begun her EMDR training in 1996, she is presently a Trainer of Trainers (EMDR Institute) and Past-President of EMDR Ibero-America (EMDR IBA, 2007-2010; 2010-2013). She is the Clinical Director of the TraumaClinic in Brasilia, Brazil, and has been directly responsible for the training of over fifteen hundred EMDR therapists in Brazil.

Other books (in English), by Esly Carvalho:

<u>**Healing the Folks Who Live Inside.**</u> Using EMDR therapy to treat our Inner Gallery of Roles has brought together the best of reprocessing and role therapy for trauma and painful memories. Written for the layperson and full of snippets from the author's case studies, it will give readers information about emotional trauma and why we should treat it. In a fun, entertaining and yet informative manner, it illustrates how our inner roles run our lives – *for better or for worse.*
https://www.createspace.com/4229106
          The purpose of this book is to help identify and clarify the existence of our Inner Gallery of roles – those who live inside all of us and that drive many aspects of our lives, such as the Scaredy-Cat, the Adolescent in Crisis, the Liar (that even lies to myself!), and the Inner Doctor. We will see how these roles are born and develop within, their functions and interactions in our lives, and how to heal the wounded ones, so that we can lead more fulfilling lives. We can also learn how to celebrate those roles that build us up and move us forward in life, and serve as positive resources when we need them. Although Role Theory is an integral part of Psychodrama the special emphasis in this healing process is on EMDR, a new reprocessing therapy developed by Dr. Francine Shapiro that was initially a form of trauma therapy. We tie together all of these aspects in order to help our Inner Gallery of roles develop "good neighborhood policies" and live in greater harmony and health.
          <u>**Bibliodrama Manual,**</u> This manual was written to help those people who are interested in developing Bibliodrama in their churches, synagogues and communities. Enriched by Peter Pitzele's midrashic form of Bibliodrama, this manual will tell you what Bibliodrama is, its form, techniques and structures, as well as suggestions for how to conduct them. Full of practical ideas and suggestions, it will guide you from simple to more advanced forms of conducting Bibliodramas. Included is how to do Playback of Biblical stories.

www.ingramcontent.com/pod-product-compliance
Lightning Source LLC
Chambersburg PA
CBHW032119280326
41933CB00009B/903